M.B.W.C.
from
E.C.
Xmas
1931.

ECS

CHRISTINA ROSSETTI

Cambridge University Press
Fetter Lane, London

New York
Bombay, Calcutta, Madras
Toronto
Macmillan

Tokyo
Maruzen Company, Ltd

CHRISTINA ROSSETTI

A STUDY

by

FREDEGOND SHOVE

ଚ୍ଚ

I will not look unto the sun
Which setteth night by night:
In the untrodden courts of heaven
My crown shall be more bright.
Lo in the New Jerusalem
Founded and built aright
My very feet shall tread on light.

CHRISTINA ROSSETTI

CAMBRIDGE
AT THE UNIVERSITY PRESS
1931

PRINTED IN GREAT BRITAIN

CONTENTS

AUTHOR'S NOTE

Although the following short study in no way pretends to be a life of Christina Rossetti, it is a matter of regret to me that it was finished before the recent biography by Miss Sandars appeared. It has therefore not been possible for me to profit by her researches as I should like to have done.

I most gratefully acknowledge the courtesy shown me by Messrs Macmillan & Co., also by the Society for Promoting Christian Knowledge, in kindly permitting me to quote from works of which they hold the copyright, and all of which are now embodied in Messrs Macmillan's edition of Christina Rossetti's Poetical Works.

F. S.

October 1930

A FOREWORD

Christina Rossetti—the name is like a song itself. Whilst my pen traces the letters that form the notes of the tuneful name the snow falls fast.

> Cold the day and cold the drifted snow,
> Dim the day until the cold dark night—

words that form the opening of January's speech about the robin in her pageant of the months—seem aptly to describe the afternoon.

I am tempted to read on and on. February will soon take up the theme:

> Brother, joy to you!
> I've brought some snowdrops; only just a few,
> But quite enough to prove the world awake,
> Cheerful and hopeful in the frosty dew
> And for the pale sun's sake.

Later April cries:

> What beaks you have, you funny things,
>   What voices shrill and weak;
> Who'd think that anything that sings
>   Could sing through such a beak?
> Yet you'll be nightingales one day,
>   And charm the country side,
> When I'm away and far away
>   And May is queen and bride.

'A Pageant', think I, as my gaze travels once more from the fragrance of these printed treasures to the snowy grass and then upwards towards the thick, light sky of a late January afternoon.

But all her poems are part of a pageant, she brings up the birds, beasts, blossoms and sounds of nature, she evokes the scents and colours of the seasons, her heart keeps tune and time with winds and waves and snowfalls, as simply as she breathes, as quietly as she sings.

Perhaps the greatest of her qualities as a poet is this extremely natural, spontaneous, heartfelt and deep resource of music.

There seems no art in the arrangement of the changeful cadences, because the art is intuitive—imagination caused it—is the tool of the highest power and therefore invisible.

It works in her soul, refining, spiritualising, crystallising and blowing ever lovelier shapes of flame or dew or frost into an ever-sweeter and intenser being:

Like the blowing of a windbringing dew.

The impulse to write poetry wrought in her fervent mind sweetly and beneficently. Her brother has suggested to us that while she certainly worked at her poems, she did not always much revise her work. Very often she wrote straight from her thought with success and without much, if any, premeditation.

It would often seem as though her desire to express something were the longing not only of a writer but of a painter and musician, mystic and lover combined.

She saw and possessed the snowdrops, lambs and

showers, transposed the liquid bird notes, at-oned
all beauty with 'God our home' and loved the whole
of innocent creation, plants, animals, souls, or star
systems with a quite stintless rapture, even with
jubilant and saintly joy akin to that of Saint
Francis of Assisi or Saint Catherine of Genoa.

But she loved God supremely and her love of
nature was always a sparkling tributary to that
boundless stiller love, so real and so personal, which
was offered in every action of her difficult, suffering
life to the Author of all goodness and all beauty.

To admire Christina Rossetti's poetry whilst remaining chill to her passionate Christianity is, I sup-
pose, possible, in a sense in which perhaps it might
not be possible to admire Francis Thompson or
George Herbert whilst objecting to or remaining
uninterested by their religion.

But I think that all such admirers of Christina
Rossetti's work are bound to lose more than half of
her message, not only of the sense but of the full
beauty and rhythmic life in it.

> When sick of life and all the world—
> How sick of all desire but Thee!—
> I lift mine eyes up to the hills,
>   Eyes of my heart that see,
> I see beyond all death and ills
> Refreshing green for heart and eyes,
> The golden streets and gateways pearled,
>   The trees of Paradise.

These melodious lines run ever parallel to the harmony in the thought, keeping tune and time with her pleasant Christian hope.

Likewise do these:

EASTER DAY

Words cannot utter
   Christ His returning:
Mankind, keep jubilee,
   Strip off your mourning,
Crown you with garlands,
   Set your lamps burning.

Speech is left speechless;
   Set you to singing,
Fling your hearts open wide,
   Set your bells ringing:
Christ the Chief Reaper
   Comes, His sheaf bringing.

Earth wakes her song-birds,
   Puts on her flowers,
Leads out her lambkins,
   Builds up her bowers:
This is man's spousal day,
   Christ's day and ours.

One who delights in 'Goblin Market', who loves 'A Birthday' and feels that in Christina Rossetti's poems for children she was sometimes most exquisitely successful because most happy, can yet not ignore that noble sequence of sonnets called 'Out of the Deep have I called unto Thee, O Lord', which contains some of the best religious poetry in the language, as well as revealing a passionate single-mindedness of devotion, an innocence and strictness of nature which should do much to enhance the reader's sense that Christina Rossetti was not only an artist, but was also a great spirit, a woman whose beautiful soul and high moral character matched all her beauty in prayer as in poetry.

Oh Lord God, hear the silence of each soul.

She utters the words as one well knowing what that silence is, how easy to break, costly to keep and fruitful when sealed with prayer. One surmises that her silences were no less full of spirituality than her songs. With all that she has ever written there breathes the fragrance and the spring-like innocence of a devout Christian. Her religion informed and invigorated all her points of view.

Pity was a ruling sentiment with her. For the cause of animals she wrote a little poem beginning:

Pity the sorrows of a poor old dog.

When she learned that the Society for the Promotion of Christian Knowledge was not (at that time at any rate) definitely antagonistic to vivisection, she refused to give it any further support.

She drew animals with delicate insight, a few slight touches, and cats, dogs, birds (especially the robin), are seen to decorate her gardens and meadows. She could not come to grief over them, and, as a dear friend of mine once said of another friend whose knowledge of birds gave her a charming manner of discoursing upon them, 'she talked as though she made them'.

> Hurt no living thing:
>   Ladybird, nor butterfly,
> Nor moth with dusty wing,
>   Nor cricket chirping cheerily,
> Nor grasshopper so light of leap,
>   Nor dancing gnat, nor beetle fat,
> Nor harmless worms that creep.

was as much a part of Christina's working creed as was her loving charity towards all humanity and the whole modest fervour of her inner life. Side by side with her keen pities went her readiness to be amused and enchanted by the play and the drollery of her animal friends. In his admirable biography of her, Mr Mackenzie Bell has told of a conversation he once had with Miss Rossetti when she asked him earnestly whether he were going away into the country 'to kill something'. Upon his answering that he never killed anything, she showed much evident relief and he felt that from that moment the friendship was properly begun upon a stable basis and could henceforth proceed without serious interruption. She afterwards told him many little things about her own cat 'Muff', showing great keenness in observation of all her habits.

Plump housekeeper dormouse has tucked himself
    neat,
Just a brown ball in moss with a morsel to eat:
Armed hedgehog has huddled him into the hedge,
While frogs scarce miss freezing deep down in the
    sedge.

But I am elaborating what is to be but a foreword to some other very slight observations, mainly drawn from the deep wells of intimate knowledge provided (in various books and at various times) by the late Mr William Rossetti, and offered as a stimulus to the quickly coming, freshly reading generation of poetry lovers of to-day. My only excuse for these digressions is that when, gazing upon the snowflakes, I began to muse about Christina Rossetti, I had a deep sense of the futility of trying to pin such a lovely thing into a foolish case, where dates and labels could but proclaim the width of the gulf lying between her and other mortals. She was meant for no museum and no 'collection'.

Most living of poets, she lives like light, like water, sound of music, scent of lilacs, lilies and roses, murmur of bees and joy of star-light. Like them, she is easy of access and free from pomp of human pride, but, like them also, it is hard, and very hard, to describe her: and to round off my foreword to this slight attempt at a recognition of Christina Rossetti's qualities as woman and as poet I cannot do better than quote the opening sentences of Mr Mackenzie Bell's sympathetic study, to which I owe a good deal of my knowledge of her life. 'Never does a writer feel so keenly how weak are words—at the best inadequate makeshifts for expressing conceptions or for conveying impressions—as when he tries to show to others in some measure the sweetness and irresistible fascination of such a personality as Christina Rossetti—a personality whose unique charm is well-nigh untranslatable into words.'

Chapter One

HER LIFE

> A lily blossoming unseen
> Holds honey in its silver cup....
> *(From 'To what Purpose is this Waste'?)*

Gabriele Rossetti and his wife Frances Mary Lavinia (Polidori), marrying in April 1826, had four children. They were: Maria Francesca, born 17 February 1827; Gabriel Charles Dante (better known as Dante Gabriel), 12 May 1828; William Michael, 25 September 1829; and Christina Georgina, 5 December 1830. These were all born at No. 38 Charlotte Street, Portland Place, London.

The memoir (by William Michael Rossetti), from which I have made the above quotation, is a model of compact information, and should be carefully studied by all who seek to make acquaintance with the fine and full edition of Christina Rossetti's poetical works to which it acts as introduction (*Poetical Works*, Macmillan). Another help to the study of the Rossetti family will be found in the preface by the same indefatigable student-brother to *Family Letters of Christina Rossetti* (Brown, Langham and Co.), and in his own *Reminiscences* (also published by Brown, Langham and Co.), which contain many precious scraps of information with regard to Christina, Maria Francesca, Dante Gabriel, and himself. The preface to the *Family Letters* contains a helpful list of dates of the principal events in the poetess's life. Both it and the *Memoir*, which is critical and extremely illuminating, should be studied together with a careful reading of the long biography by Mr Mackenzie Bell (*Christina Rossetti: a biographical and critical study*, Hurst and Blackett).

These writings, with some reading of W. M. Rossetti's *Rossetti Papers*, should suffice to give ordinary knowledge of the quiet milestones passed by Miss Rossetti, all whose adventure was of an interior and spiritual nature and all whose interest for present-day readers lies within the twin spheres of poetry and religion, not often touching the material and almost wholly divorced from the merely historical events of her day.

Christina was the youngest of her family, and one clearly gathers that her father and mother, as well as her brothers and sister, felt her to be specially cherishable. From the first she gave her mother a peculiarly warm and deeply rooted devotion. A charming series of valentines which she wrote for her bears testimony to the lyrical element in this long fragrant love.

Nevertheless, there are evidences of a kind of playfulness and literary affection between the father and his poet child.

Gabriele, the Italian political refugee, had written some poetry, the libretto for opera, and he was later to issue a book of religious verse, *L'Arpa Evangelica*: other works in prose and verse also proceeded from him around and during the years when he held his professorship of Italian at King's College, London.

Mrs Rossetti was of half-Italian parentage. Her father, Gaetano Polidori, had, however, an English home, whilst his wife was of purely English extraction. Frances Mary Lavinia Rossetti seemed to her son William to be English rather than Italian by character. She was herself a member of the Church of England and all her children were baptized within that communion.

It is nevertheless necessary to remember, whilst estimating the various traits, and in especial the mature development of Christina Rossetti's religious leanings, that Gabriele Rossetti, her father, was Catholic by baptism. There was, therefore, latent Catholicism in the blood of the Rossetti children. It is true that their father was a man of strong republican and Protestant sympathies, leaning intellectually to agnosticism and to Evangelicalism in what religion he retained. A large share of his activities and of his sympathies seems to have gone

towards defending ex-priests and Catholics of weak
faith who had turned for political or other reasons
against their Church. Nevertheless, he never actually
became a Protestant, and one cannot help feeling
about him that it was in the first instance a political
accident that precipitated his reaction against the
Catholic Church.

'He never interfered', says his son William,
'with the religious teachings of Mrs Rossetti', and
left her free to instruct the children in prayer and
catechism. They were all brought up to be believing
and practising members of the Church of England.
But the sons soon gave up going to church except
occasionally and to please their mother.

It is known, however, that when Dante Gabriel
Rossetti was in mental fever and aware that he
was about to enter upon the last stage of his illness he had at some time serious thoughts of consulting a Catholic priest. There is among his sister's
collected letters one, very touching, tremulously
sincere and humble, in which she tells him how, to
her, confession (she meant of course Anglican and
not Catholic confession) had been a great comfort, of
how she once discontinued it for a period of some
years' duration but of how, on its resumption, she
was aware of a help too precious ever to part with it
again. For to Christina, firmer in her allegiance to

their mother's teachings, the call to the older religion never seems to have come.

However this may be, one indubitable fact which emerges from the study of the Rossetti family is that every one of its richly gifted members, even to its professed agnostics (the three men Rossettis), seems to have had a good share of the religious sense. All were students of Dante, all understood religion in its enormous artistic import, its connection with every department of the life of the intellect and of the will.

Maria Rossetti bore, of course, the most deeply marked religious characteristics of the family. Her book *A Shadow of Dante* (which ran into three editions) and her subsequent entry into the Anglican sisterhood of All Saints, Margaret Street, attest to this her dominant bent—the will to serve God, the world renounced. In the National Portrait Gallery there is unfortunately no sketch or painting of this remarkable woman who exercised such a permanent and intense influence upon her still more gifted sister.

Mrs Rossetti's portrait is there (with Christina's) and what a valuable index to the study of family influence it affords! The face is somewhat that of a Roman matron. The forehead is massive, the chin round and deeply dented, the lips are firmly pleated, there are power, intellect, will, obstinacy and humour in their expression.

Christina Georgina came to have some of this heaviness, but only in later life. The pencil drawing done by Dante Gabriel Rossetti, which is to be found reproduced in *New Poems*, gives her a light loveliness as of an ethereal being stooping among shadows and sunbeams to seek the frail spring flowers she often wrote about. I like to think that this picture, of which her brother wrote that it was 'the sweetest version of her face', is also the truest likeness, for the very soul of Christina Rossetti's lyrics lives in that pale profile.

Undoubtedly the charm of this family consisted greatly in a subtle blending of Italian with English beauty. All had the full lips, dreaming eyes, broad brows and pale olive complexion now associated with so many of Dante Rossetti's pictures. In their family life there was a blending, too, of the greatly differing, strangely harmonising notes; Italian music of speech (Christina's voice and pronunciation being quite especially melodious), English reserve and depth of strong feeling; Italian sympathy for saints and their works, English love of open air (though never sport), country life and quiet; Italian intellectual precocity, English fun and sensibility to others' feelings; Italian seriousness and English childlike humour; lastly, Italian family devotion, fervent, exclusive and not unegoistic, and then English love of fair play, with devotion to animals of all kinds.

One pictures them playing in the grave and shadowy house in Charlotte Street (in 1836 they moved from 38 to 50), peeping round the bend of the staircase to catch a glimpse of some of their father's friends. Sometimes they would be seized on by Benedetto Sangiovanni, an Italian refugee who had lived in Naples under the protection of Murat and who was 'rightly or wrongly reported to have stabbed someone in Calabria'. He fascinated the children both by the glamour of this gruesomeness hanging about him and his gift of clay-modelling.

Or it might be that they would meet the painter, poor Fillippo Pistrucci, who did a water-colour of Christina when she was about seven years old, showing her to have had a very pretty, soft, plump, oval face and grey hazel eyes which seemed to contain promise of both sadness and imagination to come. Signor Pistrucci painted Maria twice, Gabriel twice, William once and Christina twice. He was helped by Gabriele Rossetti, and frequently entertained at his house, as were so many refugees and artists—indeed the thoughtful, the needy and the oppressed of all sorts and conditions of men. Scraps of a sort of conversation that is peculiarly attractive to children may have floated through the rooms of that narrow London house. It was enough to fire the young Rossettis with a bandit-like enthusiasm and it kindled in them a desire to express themselves on subjects literary, political, religious and artistic, and through the medium of rhyme and of action.

They must have seemed like a nest of young song-thrushes, vivid and eager by contrast with the sparrows and robins in most London home-trees. They sharpened their wits against one another, they glistened and quivered with song and the laughter of young minds growing an appetite for all things of beauty, stimulating each other to exercises of every lighter intellectual faculty.

To anyone coming to the house in Christina Rossetti's girlhood—the time when she was beginning to feel her way as a poet, just as Dante Gabriel was assuredly winning his through the medium of his clear, flame-like painting—the scene must have been one of a most unusual poignant attraction.

Imagine the parents, the father warmly, generously genial, the mother lovable and cultivated, sympathetic and devout. Picture the daughters, both finely built and gracious young women, one strikingly forceful and markedly, though quietly, intellectual; the other exquisite as a slim half-opened lily, with a face in which poetry lived and sparkled. Imagine the sons, the one ardent, moody by fits and starts, breaking into sentences of vivid wit and irony, showing by every word and by every look his eminence as a thinker, his promise as painter and poet; the other no less cultivated intellectually, but with a strong vein of common sense matching the Italian subtlety and keen artistic perceptions.

The Rossettis, indeed, challenge comparison with the Brontës or with any of the other gifted families in literary history. They, like the Brontës, were precocious, and although they did not live amid the fells and the snowfalls of the stark Yorkshire moors, they had a somewhat marooned existence in their dim London houses, consorting with what was peculiar in humanity, with what was often pathetic or distressed, if not with what is tragic in nature, or sinister in family life itself.

From this latter quality, a sinister element in family life, the Rossettis went free. It is true that Dante Gabriel Rossetti's life, after the tragic death of his wife through an overdose of laudanum, became an intermittent nightmare, intensified by the constant use of chloral until it deepened into night itself. But in spite of the sins, in spite of the overwhelming sorrow of that most appealing life, there seems never to have been any real estrangement between him and his family. His mother and his sister Christina (Maria Francesca did not survive him) loved their dear Gabriel tenderly and delighted in his vivid talk; he was, whenever he came to see them, the most affectionate of sons and brothers, and he came often. Christina, who nursed him in his last illness, never wavered in her loving solicitude, and the trust which she reposed in his taste and judgment with regard to all things metrical and musical is but another proof of her deep humility and of his fine intuition as to and recognition of her genius. There is surely no more striking instance of what Christianity and poetry together can do for human relationships between souls than the history of these last years of Rossetti the painter, when he leant so on his sister's love, and when her unfailing faith, whilst he could not quite attain it, served to bring an unmistakable flame of hope to his dark hours.

I have perhaps said enough to show that these six people, like six instruments, went well together and in good harmony. They harmonised and, in the true sense of the word, fraternised. Their youthful events were the writing of sonnets to bouts-rimés, the coming to the house of such men of talent as Holman Hunt, Millais, Woolner, with others of what Christina in an amusing poem has designated as 'the great

P.R.B.' (Pre-Raphaelite Brotherhood). They wrote stories or plays or poetry and they had no false modesty about the interchange of verse in letters or of drawings such as Christina did of the delicate wombat discovered by her and William at the Zoo.

There is a feeling of shy, glowing happiness about all this period of Christina's life; of an innocent, bubbling sagaciousness in important matters such as the life of *The Germ*, the P.R.B. magazine, to which she contributed some of her best poems.

One surmises that Christina Rossetti must then have been in the very flower of her loveliness. The terrible character of the illness which later came to work such havoc in her beauty and happiness was then, mercifully, only glimpsed. Anxiety had been felt, and with true cause, on the score of her health, but she was as yet happy and well enough to become engaged to be married.

In 1848, before she was eighteen, she met and grew to care for a certain member of the Pre-Raphaelite Brotherhood, called James Collinson. He had recently become a Catholic, but before he knew Christina Rossetti she had been used to notice him at services in her own church. He does not seem to have been possessed of any specially unusual qualities of charm or intellect, but his true piety and, no doubt, his connection with the great artistic adventure of Pre-Raphaelitism may have appealed to her young sense of romance.

He proposed to her twice, and the first time she rejected him, for she held with tenacity to the Anglican view in theological matters.

Thus there came about a momentary weakening of James Collinson's grip on his own religious tenets, and in order to marry Christina Rossetti he renounced for the time being the Catholic Church and became an Anglican. He then proposed to her again, and this time she accepted him. She went to stay with his people and seemed to be happy in her engagement. The affair, however, came to an end with Collinson's re-entering the Catholic Church, for Christina Rossetti felt that she could not follow him there, neither could she assent to a mixed marriage.

There are traces of Christina Rossetti's suffering at the breaking off of this young engagement in some of her letters, and there is an added touching interest about the poem which she wrote in 1852 (two years after the engagement was broken off) on Saint Elizabeth of Hungary, when we consider that she wrote it partly under the influence of James Collinson, who had painted a picture of St Elizabeth, and who had also, by rejoining the Catholic Church, put an end to the possibility of any further

relationship between himself and Christina Rossetti.

To her brother William Christina wrote that she
greatly desired to see this picture—'It must be very
beautiful', she adds wistfully. In another letter she
asks about Mr Collinson's health, and hopes that it
is better than it used to be. The letter ends thus
pathetically:

I direct this to the Excise [William Rossetti's
address at Somerset House] that Mamma may not
know of it. Do not be shocked at the concealment;
this letter would not give her much pleasure. Do
have patience both with the trouble I occasion you
and with myself. I am ashamed of this note, yet
want courage to throw it away; so must dispatch it
in its dreary emptiness with the sincere love of
Your...etc.

She seems to write with shyness and eagerness
combined, and the reader may well imagine that she
did pine long after this first love affair had come to
its close. She was not a person of weak sentiment-
alising habits, however, and there was nothing at all
morbid about the way in which she met her troubles.
Her health was very soon to give her true cause for
bitter grief, her heart was to bleed again over the
loss of her beloved brother Dante Gabriel Rossetti
and then over her mother, most beloved of all.
Lastly, she was to face the kind of mental pain which

often haunts the holier among souls when they near
the brink of death—the fear of God's justice, the
sense of deserving His most dreadful punishments.
Towards others, however, she was always markedly
indulgent—another saintly trait. She never spoke
uncharitably, and thought it a sin indeed to think
evil. Then she was not unduly narrow-minded. Her
second and by far her most serious inclination towards matrimony proves this.

In about 1860 her friendship with Charles Bagot
Cayley began. He was a brother of the well-known
mathematician and Trinity don at Cambridge and
he had been a pupil of Mr Rossetti senior, and later
became a distinguished Italian scholar. He seems to
have been a real friend as well as a devoted admirer,
and it cost Christina much to refuse his offer of
marriage. She was now between thirty and forty
and of an age to appreciate the worthy, the really
high, intellectual integrity, devoted unselfish love
and unworldly interests of a scholar. Together
they shared so many interests—animals, Italian,
literature of all kinds and card games (of which
Christina and her mother were fond). There was a
kind of rest and refreshing, unworldly strength about
Charles Cayley, and also, I think, he was more suited
to become the husband of a delicate, nervously strung
woman like Christina Rossetti than would have been

the young Catholic painter with his oscillation between religion and love. Nevertheless, as in the first,
so in the second of these two romances, religion made
a gap too serious to be bridged. Mr Cayley was a
Protestant by baptism, but by condition he belonged
rather to that group which is hazily content to be
called 'nothing in particular' and certainly does not
stand for an allegiance to any Christian sect. But
marriage with such a one, with an agnostic in fact,
would have seemed, I venture to think, to be no
marriage at all in Christina Rossetti's eyes. She refused her second suitor, and one cannot but honour
her for doing so. Afterwards they remained friends
and kept in touch with one another until Mr Cayley's death.

But we must now go back to the earlier part of
Christina Rossetti's life and follow the events which,
although slight in themselves as marking no sudden
changes of scene or of action, are most important as
indications of her modest contentment and humility,
her desire only to act, as she thought, in obedience
to duty, never shrinking away from the family environment or, so far as we know, seeming to have
much ambition beyond it. Perhaps this close love of
the family and, in particular, the beautiful veneration and devotion for the mother are especially
Italian characteristics. They were always uppermost

to the end, even when she had survived her mother and two aunts whom she nursed devotedly, and are among the strongest characteristics which she possessed.

To such a nature her home circle proved a world in miniature, and with the study of plants, beasts, books and needlework her time was filled; her days ran deep, if placidly.

What changes there are to record are chiefly changes of address; thus in 1851 the family removed from 50 Charlotte Street, Portland Place to 38 Arlington Street, Mornington Crescent, and there, being in less comfortable circumstances than formerly, Christina with Mrs Rossetti opened a small day school for children. In the spring of 1853 the plan of a school was again started and begun at Frome in Somerset, where Mrs Rossetti and Christina went to live and later were joined by Gabriele Rossetti, the rest of the family remaining in London. In 1854 William Rossetti, who was now an extra clerk in the Inland Revenue office, took a house at 166 Albany Street, where they all (except Dante Gabriel) lived together. In the same year Mr Rossetti died in that house, but his children and widow continued there until 1867 when they removed to 5 Endsleigh Gardens. In 1873 Maria Rossetti, following her strongest desires, became a novice in the Anglican Sisterhood of All Saints, Margaret Street. In 1874 William Rossetti married Lucy Madox Brown, and at first he and his wife lived under the same roof as his mother and sister. Differences of outlook (mainly perhaps religious)— which, although not provoking any want of essential affection, were yet marked as between Christina and Lucy, Lucy and her mother-in-law—made it advisable for this mode of life to be discontinued, and in 1876 Mrs Rossetti with Christina went to live at 30 Torrington Square, which they shared with Mrs Rossetti's two sisters, Eliza and Charlotte Polidori. During all these fairly frequent changes of domicile, much the same sort of even tenor of London family life seems to have flowed on and on.

At one time Miss Rossetti tried to do a little of what she called 'governessing'. But these efforts were not from her own point of view successful, since her health was early beginning to give troublesome warnings, and had soon (to her relief) to be given up.

Her visit to Penkill Castle, Scotland, to a friend, Miss Alice Boyd, lasted seven weeks and seems to have provided a time of great happiness.

She went but twice abroad, once in 1861 and again in 1865. Both journeys were accomplished under the protection of her brother William. On the first occasion they went no farther than Paris

and Normandy, returning by Jersey. The second
journey comprised visits to Basle, Como, Milan,
Freibourg and Strasburg. Christina, William and
their mother were the only members of this party.
They went over the St Gothard, and to Christina
the effect of the mountains was 'saddening'.
She did, however, write joyfully of the scene which
she saw from a window of the Schweizerhof Hotel,
Lucerne.

The mountains in their overwhelming might
  Moved me to sadness when I saw them first,
And afterwards they moved me to delight;
  Struck harmonies from silent chords which burst
  Out into song, a song by memory nursed;
For ever unrenewed by touch or sight
Sleeps the keen magic of each day or night,
  In pleasure and in wonder then immersed....

It was not Switzerland, however, that impressed
her most. Her heart was like a bulb growing in light
and love and water to quicken at the first touch of
Italian sun, and in her poem 'En Route' (dated 1865)
she cries:

Farewell, land of love, Italy,
  Sister-land of Paradise:
With mine own feet I have trodden thee,
  Have seen with mine own eyes:
I remember, thou forgettest me,
  I remember thee.

Blessed be the land that warms my heart,
　And the kindly clime that cheers,
And the cordial faces clear from art,
　And the tongue sweet in mine ears:
Take my heart, its truest tenderest part,
　Dear land, take my tears.

Of a night by Lake Como she says:

For June that night glowed like a doubled June.

'I can remember', wrote her brother, 'the intense relief and pleasure with which she saw lovable Italian faces and heard musical Italian speech at Bellinzona after the somewhat hard and nipped quality of the German Swiss.'

Christina Rossetti wrote many poems in the Italian language itself, but of these, owing to ignorance, I am unfortunately unable to speak with any but tentative appreciation.

Her love of Italy can be seen, however, in much of her English work. There is a strong tinge of it in the pretty story *Vanna's Twins*—the narrative of an Italian family living in England, in which she well caught the half-poetic, half-tragic commonplace mingling with the unconscious dignity of peasants alienated from their own warm land of beauty, and suffering a terrible shock (the loss of the twins in a snowstorm), which was brought about through the very warmth of their own compassionate hearts.

Whenever Christina Rossetti bursts into Italian we feel not so much that she is speaking her native language but that she is writing her *own* language alike in English or Italian, in both of which she was fluent and spoke with a peculiar melody, enchanting to English ears. Letters from friends and other writings give testimony to the charm of her voice and manner:

My first recollection of Christina Rossetti hovers in the sunny dreamland of earliest childhood, and in this, it may be, the ethereal grace of her rare poet's nature finds its most appropriate setting. For then it is that I have a vivid impression of playing a game of ball with her one summer afternoon upon a sloping lawn, under the branches of an old apple tree in the garden of a tiny hamlet among the Surrey hills. It was in the June of 1863 that Miss Christina Rossetti came upon her first memorable visit to my home there; she was then a dark-eyed, slender lady, in the plenitude of her poetic powers, having already written some of her most perfect poems—'Goblin Market' and 'Dream Land'.

To my child's eyes she appeared like some fairy princess who had come from the sunny south to play with me. In appearance she was Italian, with olive complexion and deep hazel eyes. She possessed, too, the beautiful Italian voice all the Rossettis were gifted with—a voice made up of strange, sweet inflexions, which rippled into silvery modulations in sustained conversation, making ordinary English words and phrases fall upon the ear with a soft, foreign, musical intonation, though she pronounced the words themselves with the purest of English accents. Most of all I used to wonder at and admire the way in which she would take up, and hold in the hollow of her hand, cold little frogs and clammy toads, or furry many-legged caterpillars, with a fearless love that we country children could never emulate. Even to the individual whisk of one squirrel's tail from another's, or to the furtive scuttle of a rabbit across a field or common, nothing escaped her nature-loving ken; yet her excursions into the country were as angels' visits, 'few and far between'; but when there, how much she noted of flower and tree, beast and bird!

This extract is from an article in *Good Words* written by Mrs Frend, who was a daughter of Miss Rossetti's greatest friend Anne Gilchrist.[1] I choose it rather than a good many others to quote in full, since it touches on so many graceful and original points concerning the poetess's habits and appearance. We must, whilst trying to study her, never forget the very ardent and unaffected spirituality which translated itself into such simple and loving handling of all her fellow-creatures.

In *Time Flies* she moralises quite naturally but most reverently over a centipede that once crept into her room at Penkill Castle when she was staying with Miss Boyd. Her drawings from animals seen at the Zoo show a joyful life, and her letters abound in

[1] It is quoted by Mr Mackenzie Bell in his *Christina Rossetti* (p. 38). Mrs Gilchrist's husband was Blake's biographer.

references to pets kept either by her brother Dante Gabriel or other of her friends and relatives. It is noticeable, too, that these affections of Christina were not only affairs of the heart. She kept seaweed and sea animals in her room and was very fond, as may be seen in *Commonplace* and *The Waves of this troublesome World* (two of her short stories), of pacing the beach in search of the treasures that the waves cast up, which kept a childish glamour for her always. All creatures, then, the sea, plants of all kinds and the fruit or blossom of common hedgerow and bank played their parts with devout intensity in the inward drama of this homely and spiritual genius. All through the events of her life—two frustrated loves, the painful bereavements, the often still more painful anxieties for loved human beings, and lastly the shattering illness—she was ever ready to be cheerful and instructed by the beauty of humble creatures, dusty coated or husk-contained, green and varnished or brightly glazed, winged, shelled or coated, furred or feathered, mewing or barking; so long as they were animals (not goblins or people disguised as animals), she protected them and they protected her. She never in all her life refused comforts offered by these frail people. Hobbies and distractions to others, the smallest of natural phenomena were a part of her spiritual equipment; and if anyone

doubts it, let him read her prose devotional work
Called to be Saints, where she finds for each of the
saints in the Book of Common Prayer his or her appropriate plant or precious stone; or let him have
recourse to *Time Flies*, also a diary of saints and
apostles, drawn this time from a larger calendar and
which abounds in little stories about dogs, grass-
hoppers, spiders, frost, dew and sunlight. In this, as in
all her other works, we find the same reverent attitude to nature, and yet it is not like Wordsworth's
reverent attitude, still less like that of Rousseau.
It has nothing of the cultus about it. It is rooted,
one feels, in her interests and her homeliness, her very
self has struck root in the heart of this heavenly
home our earth, seen spiritually as a portent, never
as an end or even only as a beginning; since the
beginning came, as the end will come, in the mind
of the Creator.

It seems to me that Christina Rossetti is almost
unique in this special simplicity, reality, this effort-
less, unpretending acceptance together with true
delight in all the works of God.

Perhaps it will be seen from the very slight
sketch here given of her life and environment that
while, doubtless, she deepened and strengthened,
she did not actually change very much. Events of
such a fundamentally uprooting nature as those

which made Elizabeth Barrett Browning a creature
of two hemispheres—of a before and of an after as
it were—never came to shake the foundations or to
cleave the affections of this outwardly tranquil
existence. Such disturbances had George Eliot's life,
George Sand's also; and even Charlotte Brontë
seems never, after she had achieved the height of her
fame as a novelist, to have been quite the same
woman. Christina Rossetti, on the other hand, knew
no sudden blaze of literary glory. She made no
holocaust of some uncongenial home or hearth or
faith or father or husband. She never stepped into
the artificial brilliance of what is called a literary
career. To her, literary success came soon; her first
book *Goblin Market and other Poems* brought it in
some measure and steadily her poetic reputation
grew, but it was a wholesome growth and does not
seem to have given her over-much concern, for, while
she took her gift seriously, she seems to have been
unattacked by the poison of artistic ambition, un-
molested by a desire to dazzle, while yet never
morbidly shrinking from legitimate success.

In 1850 (January to May) she published various
poems in the magazine started by the Pre-Raphaelite
Brotherhood called *The Germ*. These were her first
publications, excepting two pieces which had appeared in the *Athenæum*. In 1847, however, when

she was but seventeen years old, a small book of her verses had been privately printed by her grand-father, Gaetano Polidori. Among these verses one 'On the death of a cat, a friend of mine aged ten and a half' will doubtless be familiar to my readers. It has a certain sedate grace and neatness, as have other of these poems, which yet do not foreshadow the real poetic beauty to come so very soon to the summit of its glory with the volume of 1862. In this book was 'Goblin Market', a poem of such extraordinary freshness and colour, such glowing imagination, above all so much music that it could not fail to charm, even to startle, for nothing at all like it had yet been before the reading public. (The poems of Dante Gabriel Rossetti were, it will be remembered, not to appear in book form before the year 1870— his lovely 'Blessed Damozel' having also been printed in *The Germ*.)

Illustrated with sympathetic insight by Dante Gabriel Rossetti himself, this poem and its com-panions brought the instant attention of the literary world to its authoress. 'Miss Rossetti', wrote a *Times* reviewer, 'can point to work which could not easily be mended.' This inspired remark drew a pencil sketch from Dante Gabriel Rossetti which is sent in a letter to his sister. It represents Christina armed with a hammer destroying her household furniture. Despite the mild tone of the reviews, however, there is a quite perceptible note of excitement and a certain welcoming pleasure (notwithstanding the familiar tone of slight patronage) which indicates the inclination of the world to enjoy such pure, undidactic poetry as this. Her devotional verse too, some of which came out in this first volume, evoked sympathetic remark.

It is amusing enough at this date to look back upon such a letter as the following one from the great critic of art and letters—John Ruskin—written after reading many of the poems included in this volume (as yet unpublished):

DEAR ROSSETTI,

I sate up till late last night reading poems. They are full of beauty and power. But no publisher— I am deeply grieved to know this—would take them, so full are they of quaintnesses and offences.

Irregular measure (introduced to my great regret, in its chief wilfulness, by Coleridge) is the calamity of modern poetry.

*　　　*　　　*　　　*

Your sister should exercise herself in the severest commonplace of metre until she can write as the public like. Then if she puts in her observation and passion all will become precious. But she must have the form first.

There can be no reasonable doubt that Christina Rossetti was pleased with her self-evident success, pleased as only a really modest person can be. She never expected a great deal of notice, and seriously as she took her writing, she was always ready to put it aside to render some often quite small service to those belonging to her, or to the poor, or to the unfortunate. The laughing references in her letters to 'Mac' (her publisher) and to the gentlemen and ladies desirous to set her songs to music are indications of the manner in which, while prizing her gift, she at all times refused to take herself pompously.

In 1866 she brought out her second volume, *The Prince's Progress and other Poems*. She was now well started in her career as a poetess and quietly as she lived, unpretentious as she was, the qualities displayed in her second volume being in no way behind those for which the first was remarkable, she had now only bright things to look for in the literary world. For the appeal which she made was to more than one type of mind, as will be seen by the most cursory glance at the list of her acquaintances during this time. To name but a few of the distinguished men and women with whom she came into touch during the ensuing years, one might mention Professor Masson, Edmund Gosse, Robert Browning (Mrs Browning she never met), Canon Burrows, Canon Dickson, the poet, William Bell Scott, Jean Ingelow, Dora

Greenwell, William Sharp, Mrs Cameron, Mr Watts
Dunton, Algernon Charles Swinburne, William
Morris and his wife, Ruskin, Coventry Patmore,
Prebendary Glendinning Nash (her clergyman in
later years), Miss Henrietta Rintoul, Dr Littledale,
Sir William Jenner (her consulting physician) and
Mr Mackenzie Bell (later to be her biographer); and
these are but a selection from the names given by
Mr William Rossetti in his memoirs of his sister. All
were then names of significance and in some special
sense of distinction in their day.

In 1871, after various illnesses which had come and
gone in fits and starts since her fifteenth year, Christina Rossetti underwent a severe strain and shock.
She was now at the height of her powers and in a
modest way may be said to have had a fair measure
of fulfilment, the happiness of an artist in her work-
shop surrounded by congenial, familiar, dear and
homely things and people, enlivened by occasional
glimpses of the most delightful society to be had,
that of good and intelligent people, amusing and
genuine friends. But in this year 1871 a great trial
came to her and it took her whole spiritual strength
to meet it. She was prostrated by a terrible illness—
Dr Graves' disease (exophthalmic bronchocele). It
may as well be said here as anywhere, and in a true
account of Miss Rossetti's life it should be said, that

this illness is supposed to be one which causes a definitely neurasthenic outlook—and by some it has even been suggested that the illness itself is in some degree, however slight, the basis of all neurasthenic disorders. These considerations may help to explain the depressed condition of Christina Rossetti's mind during the latter part of her life, although indeed the pain she endured and the narcotics to which she was obliged to have recourse would be amply sufficient to account for much depression.

She suffered, as she did all things, with great serenity and dignity. Her lovely face and graceful figure were affected by the illness, her throat and eyes, her whole appearance painfully altered. In one or two places she comments calmly on this. She speaks of her 'fearful brownness', her altered handwriting, and seems to be without the irritation of sensitive self-consciousness which would have magnified these symptoms in other people's eyes. Indeed, although Christina Rossetti's poetry has quite often been criticised as morbid, I find a most unmorbid matter-of-fact acceptance of pain, sickness and the prospect of death or of old age to have been her strong characteristic throughout these trying years, when she could never be certain as to how ill or how well she was to feel on any given occasion, and when rules of diet and rules of rest were to pre-

clude all refreshing change and variety of occupation
in life. That she was often weary to the brink of
being in despair, often fretted, often hungry for
beautiful days of sunlight, youth and ease, such as
she knew she had done with, we have only to turn to
many of her writings to see. And yet in spite of all
this weariness, distaste and exhaustion, Christina
Rossetti had joy in giving, joy in enduring, joy in
loving still. Her already deep spirituality could but
be deepened by the bearing of such a cross as hers.
She lived henceforth for and with her Lord and
Master, Jesus Christ. We may search her letters
through and find very little indication of this hidden
life, but it shines through and illumines all her poems,
whether devotional or secular.

For her there was never any question as to how
the individual soul should meet its chiefest ills. She
was Christian to the core and marrow of her being
and Christianity sustained her where all else would
have failed.

In 1873 this illness was temporarily subdued, and,
in spite of the misery it had caused and the occasional
threatenings of danger, it seemed at that moment as
if there was some reason to hope for better things.
Her heart, however, remained in a state of chronic
weakness and the condition of her health could
never be relied upon.

In 1876 Maria Francesca Rossetti died in the Anglican convent of All Saints, Margaret Street. Her death was much felt by her sister, but it was felt, I imagine, more as a beautiful than as a sad event; it was an earnest of much hope. For her elder sister Christina had almost a veneration, she certainly always treasured her words and her advice. In the *Face of the Deep* and in *Time Flies* several of Maria's sayings are quoted with reverence although, of course, her name is not given. In one such instance Christina Rossetti speaks of her sister as 'a dear saint'.

In 1882 Dante Gabriel's tragic life ended. Next year Christina lost her much-loved friend Charles Cayley, and in 1886 her mother died. Christina Rossetti continued to live quietly at the house in Torrington Square with her two old aunts, Charlotte and Eliza Polidori, whose respective deaths occurred in 1890 and in 1893. Her own life was now definitely under sentence, for in 1892 she had to undergo an operation for cancer on the left side of the chest. She met this trial with great fortitude, and as the operation was both skilfully and successfully performed by Mr Lawson, the surgeon, she was able to some extent still to rally and to continue her conversations with friends, her reading and other tranquil occupations. She knew, however, that she

could never really be well again, and indeed so soon
as August, 1894, she was once for all confined to her
bed. There was a fresh outbreak of the cancer, and
this time no operation could be performed owing to
dropsy in the left arm which complicated the whole
terrible illness.

Her last months are wonderful even to think of.
She was uncomplaining and very gentle. She had
lived a completely unpretentious, selfless and most
useful life. She was a true poet, a finished artist, a
beautiful and accomplished person, but she had lived
in great seclusion, simply because she had no worldly
desires or ambitions. When death approached, she
shrank from the punishments which she thought she
deserved. In spite of her deep Christian love, under
the stress of great physical pain and in that dimming
of hope which long and grave illness involves, she
seemed to lie in the shadows, patiently awaiting the
striking of some awful rod and the sound of some
terrible, because much-loved accents, saying 'De-
part'. With her close knowledge of both Testaments,
her literal and Dantesque clearness of vision, her
deep sense of abasement and humility before the
Judge of all mankind, it could hardly have been
otherwise. Saints are those who tremble at the
awful thought of God's displeasure. Christina Rossetti loved the saints. She would have been con-

sumed with fear and awe at anyone suggesting that
she was herself one of their company. Nevertheless
we may like to imagine her so if we choose. All
her life she strained upward to God ('Struggling,
panting up to God', as she cried): her music was the
breath of the things turned towards God: her heart
never ceased praising; even when literally it burned
with the pain in her breast, it still praised. She was
like Saint Teresa of Avila, an artist caught and en-
raptured in the starry chains of her heavenly adventure. Her Holy Communion was her hour of
repose with Jesus: she was in Heaven when the
Saviour came to meet her at that mysterious moment
of her mystical union and could write:

> Lo now Thy banner over me is love,
> All heaven flies open to me at Thy nod,

or again:

> Tune me, O Lord, into one harmony
>   With Thee, one full responsive vibrant chord;
> Unto Thy praise, all love and melody,
>   Tune me, O Lord.

And we know that when she died on 29th December, 1894, she was in a state of prayer that lasted
some hours, only her lips moving, her head constantly inclined at the moment when she said
'Jesus'.

It may seem to some that the last years of

Christina Rossetti's life, lived as they were alone
except for the two faithful maid servants who lived
with her and, of course, latterly with her nurse, must
have been melancholy ones, though even a cursory
knowledge of the poet's vivid imagination would
preclude anyone from supposing them to have been
in the least dreary. She was then dependent upon
much help, she was also compelled to do less—to
imagine, therefore, with even more concentration—
and she had, as we have seen, a tendency to scrupu-
losity and to brooding upon her own deficiencies—
'sins' in her own meek view. Still, I think we may
confidently assume that there was a basis of stability
and reasonable everyday cheerfulness in all the hours
and even the sufferings of these last months which
made them more than bearable, gladly acceptable
to Christina herself. Her brother was much struck
by her nobility of bearing during the last talks he
had with her. Mr Mackenzie Bell could never forget
the beautiful repose he saw in the face of the dead
Christina. Her nurse, her clergyman and doctors all
carried away the impression of sweetness and
sanctity which are real and can only be won in labour
and effort by souls of unusual dispositions.

Now that it is thirty-six years since her body was
laid in the grave at Highgate Cemetery on a pale but
not cold winter day such as she would have loved,

her tender virtues, together with her songs, give fragrant greeting to all who seek to know her better, whether among the letters, so calm as almost to seem commonplace, or in the frequent glimpses to be found in other works of the day, reminiscence or biography. But as the true chronicle of her life and her heart is embedded in Christina Rossetti's poems, her little-known stories and prose devotional compilations, it is now time to pass on from the review of the actual time which she spent upon earth to that of the place which she undoubtedly fills in the region of artistic immortality.

Chapter Two

HER POEMS

There grows a tree from ancient root
With healing leaves and twelvefold fruit
In musical heaven-air:
Feast with me there.
(*From 'A Shadow of Dorothea'*)

Hitherto we have been trying to form a certain image (albeit a faint one) of Christina Rossetti's character as it was revealed in her quiet heroic life, her sufferings, her sympathies and her religious strength. It is now time to begin to look at her poetry and to consider its claims to greatness. In doing this, I shall not adhere to any close following of her work in co-ordination with the dates of the first editions which were issued. Anyone who wants to study the poems chronologically has only to resort to the three excellent appendices contained in the volume of her collected works edited by William Michael Rossetti.

I have already said something of the impression made by 'Goblin Market' when it appeared in 1862. It is a poem which shows most clearly Christina Rossetti's unusual powers of visualisation. The description of the maidens, of the fruit and of the goblins are things of astonishing vigour. They seem

to spring straight from Christina Rossetti's soul,
carried on an uprush of creative energy, with brilliant and fantastic inspiration and without the
smallest strain. Strain, affectation or staleness would
most quickly have been apparent in a poem of this
kind, but the colours in this artist's box were never
stale. She was mistress of every pure, keen tint, from
spring's rash green to autumn's damson hue, and
with her beautiful eye for colour went an exquisite
ear for melody. But these gifts could not have
accounted for 'Goblin Market' without the presence
of a third—her actual imagination, which delighted
in the delineation of the grotesque beings, seized
their pace, apprehended their gait, their speech, their
demeanour and their awful spiritual significance. As
soon as we begin to listen for them we are thrilled by
a sense of the eerie, of the fairy world:

> Down the glen tramp little men.
> One hauls a basket,
> One bears a plate,
> One lugs a golden dish
> Of many pounds' weight.

So that we are in a mood to be gratified rather
than surprised when we read more of the goblins:

> Laughed every goblin
> When they spied her peeping:
> Came towards her hobbling,
> Flying, running, leaping,

Puffing and blowing,
Chuckling, clapping, crowing,
Clucking and gobbling,
Mopping and mowing,
Full of airs and graces,
Pulling wry faces,
Demure grimaces,
Cat-like and rat-like,
Ratel- and wombat-like,
Snail-paced in a hurry,
Parrot-voiced and whistler,
Helter skelter, hurry skurry,
Chattering like magpies,
Fluttering like pigeons,
Gliding like fishes,—

And here it may be worth while to mention that these goblin men, while they assume animal voices, are not meant to be confused with the animals they simulate. Indeed, the expressions 'cat-like' and 'wombat-like' are used. They were fairies of evil origin and they could doubtless, had they wished it, have appeared under human guise. The beautiful girls whom they tried to tempt with fruit, succeeding in Lizzie's case, whereas in Laura's they failed, are lovingly and exquisitely described; but so great is the art with which the whole picture is done that there is nothing at all ugly even about the goblin men as Christina Rossetti portrays them. The poem throughout is vaguely symbolic, but throughout it is kept in fairy-tale tone. (Christina Rossetti herself said that it had no hidden allegorical meaning.) The dappled magic of an old country tale of warning to maidens not to play with the fruits of evil or witch-craft has dyed it through and through. This must have been a difficult feat to achieve, but it is done with no appearance of anything but a story-teller's full measure of ease and pleasant mystery. If we turn to the horrible passage in Spenser's *Faerie Queene* where the monster swallows and then dis-gorges her young, we shall see how it is possible to bring in too much of the human sense of horror to a fairy scene, where horror is the more keenly felt for being married to the strange unreal beauty. Coleridge in his ' Christabel ' or his ' Ancient Mariner ' understood how to do this, but even his methods seem obvious by comparison with Christina Rossetti. He is a little deliberately gruesome, inclined to over-emphasise the glittering of the moon or the wild-ness in the lady's eyes. In ' Kubla Khan ' he achieves at one stroke what he could not always do in fifty.

> The shadow of the dome of pleasure
> Floated midway on the waves;
> Where was heard the mingled measure
> From the fountain and the caves.

Even if she never touched these heights of sug-gestive evocation, Christina Rossetti had some of the power that can, through an extremely subtle rhythm, coupled with a highly sensitive collection of words, manage to convey a whole realm of shadowy and haunted beauty hid within the one whose actual tones and colours are the immediate subject of a poem.

> Lilies upon the surface, deep below
> Two wistful faces craving each for each.

These lines in 'An Echo from Willow-wood' show some of this power, as do several in 'The Hour and the Ghost', that strange poem written early on in her life when she seems, like her brother Dante Gabriel, to have dwelt much upon the thought of apparitions and spirits returning from the dead.

Akin to 'Goblin Market' in that it is a narrative poem of length and vivid beauty is 'The Prince's Progress'. It has the metrical distinction of all the author's best work and the rhymes in it are most skilfully arranged, for there are but two in each stanza, the order of them being as follows: *aaabab*. It is true that this metre was, even for Christina Rossetti, a dangerous one, and she sometimes brings in for the sake of a rhyme a word which does strike one as clumsy and unwelcome; but this does not often happen, since she had an amazingly good vocabulary as well as an inborn sense of the fitness of words which is quite one of her most enviable gifts.

The story of 'The Prince's Progress' is not so fresh nor so original as that of 'Goblin Market', but it gave scope for some very lovely writing; and the pictures of wild, desolate or fertile and watery lands through which the laggard prince travelled to find his princess are finely conceived, whilst the description of his meeting with an old sorcerer who is boiling a pot of seething herbs has the same touch of magic about it that makes the goblins really uncanny. The sorcerer's death is related in terse, almost humorously vibrating language, rougher and pithier than readers of some of the poetess' work would have believed possible.

> Thus at length the old crab was nipped.
> The dead hand slipped, the dead finger dipped
> In the broth as the dead man slipped:—
>   That same instant, a rosy red
> Flushed the steam, and quivered and clipped
>   Round the dead old head.

And so the prince, taking his phial of the elixir of life, goes flying into strange countries and is almost drowned in a whirlpool, but he is rescued by one with

> Oh a moon face in a shadowy place,
> And a light touch and a winsome grace,
> And a thrilling tender voice which says:
>   'Safe from waters that seek the sea'.

He reaches the bride's palace at length, but just as he is going into its golden gates he is met by the bier on which his princess lies dead of grief, carried by veiled and chanting figures:

> 'Ten years ago, five years ago,
>   One year ago,
> Even then you had arrived in time,
>   Though somewhat slow;
> Then you had known her living face
>   Which now you cannot know:
> The frozen fountain would have leaped,
>   The buds gone on to blow,
> The warm south wind would have awaked
>   To melt the snow.'

The poor prince has brought roses, but he is told that they are 'too red,' and pale poppies are strewn on the dead bride.

Next in order of likeness to these two long poems, 'A Royal Princess' might suggest itself, as bearing by subject (a royal and beautiful being), by its similarity of metre, length and the certain affinity to a ballad that it shows, some resemblance to 'The Prince's Progress'. It is the story of a princess who owns every luxury. One evening she says:

I took my bath of scented milk, delicately waited on:
They burned sweet things for my delight, cedar and
  cinnamon,
They lit my shaded silver lamp, and left me there
  alone.

A day went by, a week went by. One day I heard
    it said:
'Men are clamouring, women, children, clamouring
    to be fed;
Men like famished dogs are howling in the streets for
    bread'.

The princess goes to her window and sees the crowd.
She takes her 'ransom' in her hands, descends and
gives it to the hungry people. This poem was written
in 1861, and a year later it appeared in a magazine
which was contrived specially to raise funds for the
starving cotton-spinners of Lancashire, who were
out of work on account of the civil war then raging
in the United States. It is very dramatic, and I know
of no one of Christina Rossetti's poems which sets
out to be dramatic and fails. Sometimes she only
writes a little drama, sometimes it is the fragment
of a great and bitter one such as that which is limned
in the short tragic poem 'Maude Clare':

    Out of the church she followed them
      With a lofty step and mien:
    His bride was like a village maid,
      Maude Clare was like a queen.

    'Son Thomas,' his lady mother said,
      With smiles, almost with tears:
    'May Nell and you but live as true
      As we have done for years;

'Your father thirty years ago
　　Had just your tale to tell;
But he was not so pale as you,
　　Nor I so pale as Nell.'

My lord was pale with inward strife,
　　And Nell was pale with pride;
My lord gazed long on pale Maude Clare
　　Or ever he kissed the bride.

'Lo, I have brought my gift, my lord,
　　Have brought my gift,' she said:
'To bless the hearth, to bless the board,
　　To bless the marriage-bed.

'Here's my half of the golden chain
　　You wore about your neck,
That day we waded ankle-deep
　　For lilies in the beck.

'Here's my half of the faded leaves
　　We plucked from budding bough,
With feet amongst the lily leaves,—
　　The lilies are budding now.'

He strove to match her scorn with scorn,
　　He faltered in his place:
'Lady,' he said,—'Maude Clare,' he said,—
　　'Maude Clare':—and hid his face.

She turned to Nell: 'My Lady Nell,
　　I have a gift for you;
Though, were it fruit, the bloom were gone,
　　Or, were it flowers, the dew.

'Take my share of a fickle heart,
  Mine of a paltry love:
Take it or leave it as you will,
  I wash my hands thereof.'

'And what you leave,' said Nell, 'I'll take,
  And what you spurn I'll wear;
For he's my lord for better and worse,
  And him I love, Maude Clare.

'Yea though you're taller by the head,
  More wise, and much more fair,
I'll love him till he loves me best—
  Me best of all, Maude Clare.'

I come now to 'Maiden Song', one of the most successful of her narrative poems. It is a kind of simple fairy tale, the story of three sisters, two of whom went wandering into the spring meadows to find their happy fates awaiting them, whilst the third and fairest waited at home and is sought in marriage by a king. In the treatment of their beauty, the beauty of the daylight, the flowers, the sunlight deepening, the moon-rise, and the joy of the maidens in their innocent loves, there is a magical freshness, unequalled by any other of the authoress's poems. No hint of sorrow, pain or weariness is present. The whole is a picture of joy, most difficult of all atmospheres to present because so easily confused with commonplace cheerfulness and mechanical liveliness.

Had Miss Rossetti been less fragile, had she been less well acquainted with pain and conflict, she could hardly have achieved such work as this:

> The slope was lightened by her eyes
>> Like summer lightning fair,
> Like rising of the haloed moon
>> Lightened her glimmering hair,
> While her face lightened like the sun
>> Whose dawn is rosy white.
> Thus crowned with maiden majesty
>> She peered into the night,
> Looked up the hill and down the hill,
>> To left hand and to right,
> Flashing like fire-flies to and fro.

Such delicacy is the especial reward of those whose very sensitiveness to the weary and distasteful task of bearing pain and disappointment secretly renders them able to rise eagerly to meet the sunshine and the sweetness of the fields in the early morning. What lovelier picture could heart desire than this of the maiden who stayed at home while her two sisters set out to look for

> Strawberry leaves and May-dew
>> In brisk morning air?

> So these two fair sisters
>> Went with innocent will
> Up the hill and down again,
>> And round the homestead hill:
> While the fairest sat at home,
>> Margaret like a queen,

> Like a blush-rose, like the moon
>   In her heavenly sheen,
> Fragrant-breathed as milky cow
>   Or field of blossoming bean,
> Graceful as an ivy bough
>   Born to cling and lean;
> Thus she sat to sing and sew.

Here the natural liveliness, later much dimmed by ill-health and mental warfare, suggests and keeps pace with the bright, stepping metre. The words are sweet and daring. The comparison of the maiden's breath to a cow's has that innocent unconventionality and born surety of touch that are among Christina Rossetti's special notes. No other poet of her era has this kind of absolutely unpremeditated boldness of fancy. All through the poem there are notes of the same exquisite purity and sweetness:

> When Meggan pluckt the thorny rose,
>   And when May pulled the brier,
> Half the birds would swoop to see,
>   Half the beasts drew nigher,
> Half the fishes of the streams
>   Would dart up to admire.
> But, when Margaret pluckt a flag-flower
>   Or poppy hot aflame,
> All the beasts and all the birds
>   And all the fishes came
> To her hand more soft than snow.

It would be pleasant to dwell longer on these brightest poems, on 'Goblin Market' with its unrivalled richness and exquisite brilliance of fancy, on 'The Prince's Progress' opening wild suggestive landscapes before us, or on 'Maiden Song' so gay and china-fresh with its touch of an earthly paradise, an eternal arcadia of dew and sunshine. But I must now consider Christina Rossetti in her capacity as sonneteer, turning to the well-known sonnet sequence called 'Monna Innominata' which has been so much compared to Mrs Browning's *Sonnets from the Portuguese* and was indeed partially inspired by these poems, which Christina Rossetti much admired. In a prefatory note she alludes gracefully to Mrs Browning whom she styles 'the great poetess of our own day'.

These sonnets ('Monna Innominata'), called after some imaginary and forgotten Italian lady, bear really, of course, the impress of Christina Rossetti's own heart. Here and there she seems actually to lift the veil of her sensitive reticence and to show us a glimpse of that inner and heartrending struggle between inclination and what seemed to her to be duty which was then going on in her life. Read without biographical reference, however, the sonnets, though dignified and always indicative of a nobly sensitive, fastidiously high-minded nature, do not bear the stamp of her highest talent and cannot be rated with her best purely lyrical work. I choose out the last

as possibly the finest of the fourteen pieces, and
certainly it does stand up alone without the upholstery of human association as a thing of considerable might and depth:

Youth gone, and beauty gone if ever there
   Dwelt beauty in so poor a face as this;
   Youth gone and beauty, what remains of bliss?
I will not bind fresh roses in my hair,
To shame a cheek at best but little fair,—
   Leave youth his roses, who can bear a thorn,—
I will not seek for blossoms anywhere,
   Except such common flowers as blow with corn.
Youth gone and beauty gone, what doth remain?
   The longing of a heart pent up forlorn,
     A silent heart whose silence loves and longs;
     The silence of a heart which sang its songs
   While youth and beauty made a summer morn,
Silence of love that cannot sing again.

Among the religious sonnets also there are some
lasting contributions to this form of lyric poetry.

Come, blessed sleep, most full, most perfect, come:
   Come, sleep, if so I may forget the whole;
   Forget my body and forget my soul,
Forget how long life is and troublesome.
Come, happy sleep, to soothe my heart or numb,
   Arrest my weary spirit or control:
   Till light be dark to me from pole to pole,
And winds and echoes and low songs be dumb.
Come, sleep, and lap me into perfect calm,
   Lap me from all the world and weariness:

Come, secret sleep, with thine unuttered psalm,
　　Safe sheltering in a hidden cool recess:
　　Come, heavy dreamless sleep, and close and press
Upon mine eyes thy fingers dropping balm.

It is impossible not to think of Sir Philip Sidney's

　　Come, Sleep; O Sleep! the certain knot of peace.

But Christina Rossetti's genius was too lyrical ever
for contentment with a sonnet. The sonnet is a kind
of solidified lyricism, it is a nugget of rich ore, the
lyric pure and liquid is free and easy of metre. Let
us turn to one of the loveliest in the world, written
when Miss Rossetti was but eighteen years old:

　　　　　When I am dead, my dearest,
　　　　　　Sing no sad songs for me;
　　　　　Plant thou no roses at my head,
　　　　　　Nor shady cypress tree:
　　　　　Be the green grass above me
　　　　　　With showers and dewdrops wet:
　　　　　And if thou wilt, remember,
　　　　　　And if thou wilt, forget.

　　　　　I shall not see the shadows,
　　　　　　I shall not feel the rain;
　　　　　I shall not hear the nightingale
　　　　　　Sing on as if in pain:
　　　　　And dreaming through the twilight
　　　　　　That doth not rise nor set,
　　　　　Haply I may remember,
　　　　　　And haply may forget.

A thing so perfect in form, coming to so exquisite a conclusion and bearing no trace of any flaw or effort, is as rare as a beautiful face with an unchangingly lovely expression. It was written by a girl of eighteen and it sets the mark of literary excellence really transcending the average work of her time.

With Tennyson, Swinburne, the Brownings, Matthew Arnold, William Morris and more lately with Coventry Patmore, Jean Ingelow, George Meredith, Alice Meynell, Dora Greenwell, Katharine Tynan and many more, the middle years of Queen Victoria's reign were productive of a rich crop of poets and poetesses of various and brilliant merit: but among them all it is assuredly to Christina Rossetti that the highest place among lyrists must be given. And if she be accorded (perhaps rightly) a lesser share of the power of dramatic story-telling than Tennyson, a slighter intellectual equipment than the Brownings, a fainter because a more diffused imagination than that of her brother, Dante Gabriel, in respect of music, if music be the test, she comes out (at her best) ahead of Tennyson himself, complete as was his mastery of the science of prosody.

Swinburne said in praise of Herrick that his best work was akin to Miss Rossetti's, and it is with the Elizabethan lyrists and the mystics of the seventeenth century that her soul has kinship, whatever her art may have derived from Tennyson or Mrs Browning. One feels that Webster's famous lines:

> Call for the robin-redbreast and the wren,
> Since o'er shady groves they hover,
> And with leaves and flowers do cover
> The friendless bodies of unburied men.
> Call unto his funeral dole
> The ant, the field-mouse, and the mole...,

and his first line:

> All the flowers of the spring

might be Christina Rossetti's, hardly anyone else's.

In her little masque 'The Months: a Pageant'— *A Pageant and other Poems* was the title of her third volume of poetry issued in 1881—Christina Rossetti had scope for some lyrical work which, whilst not quite ever touching the isolated songs, did show off her gift to a very great advantage. The work is late and it shows great ease and mastery and has the dramatic power of which the 'Ballad of Boding', 'From House to Home', 'The Prince's Progress', 'Maiden Song' and others will have shown a greater share. But its charms are descriptive and suggestive.

The characters of the 'Pageant' are the twelve months in the year. Each comes in, speaks his or her part and, being joined by the month who is to succeed him, retires. The thread of the story is thus of the slenderest, but the nature of it demands

variety and each month's separate utterance provides an excellent excuse for changes in metre and
for giving the audience those little glimpses of the
fleeting year which exactly suited the poet's gift for
elegant fashioning and spontaneous diction. These
lines of March are reminiscent of Shelley's 'Cloud':

> I blow an arouse
> Through the world's wide house
> To quicken the torpid earth:
> Grappling I fling
> Each feeble thing,
> But bring strong life to the birth.
> I wrestle and frown,
> And topple down;
> I wrench, I rend, I uproot;
> Yet the violet
> Is born where I set
> The sole of my flying foot,

[Hands violets and anemones to February, who
retires into the background.]

> And in my wake
> Frail wind-flowers quake,
> And the catkins promise fruit....

The wind-flowers and the violets belong to Miss
Rossetti, wherever the wind has come from that
blew them hither. April says:

> Birth means dying,
> As wings and wind mean flying....

And May:

> Here are my buds of lily and of rose,
>   And here's my namesake blossom may;
>   And from a watery spot
>   See here forget-me-not,
>   With all that blows
>   To-day.

June says:

> Indeed I feel as if I came too soon
> To round your young May moon....

July has:

> Blue flags, yellow flags, flags all freckled...

and so on. Each has an original gift to make, and with each in turn we think this is the most beautiful of all the months. December ends the 'Pageant' with a lyric of which the closing lines are:

> For I've a carol which some shepherds heard
> Once in a wintry field.

We must go straight back to the earlier English poets to match the simple earnestness and childlike wonder of that.

The volume called *Sing Song* (published in 1872) was intended for children, and if the testimony of one child who loved it dearly be sufficient to show which way opinions were likely to flow, it had indeed an appreciative public. I well remember the pale silky green cover, veined like a young beech leaf, with its golden edges—I still cherish the memory of the drawings done by Arthur Hughes which embellished that first edition of *Sing Song*, a copy of which it was our childish privilege to receive. There was something about the drawings and the poems together which partook, not of fairyland, but of the enchantment of life itself—indescribable as a sea of changing colours touching all the shores of possibility. In this sea one paddled comfortably and easily, as one learnt by heart the phrases in *Sing Song*, aware all the time that whilst one was never out of one's depth, that was not because there were no depths, no soundless mystery of poetic wonder in which to bathe if one wished to do so later on, in the distant grown-up days. Now, in my grown-up days, I have come to the conclusion that these artless poems of childhood and for childhood do indeed evince a sort of immensity of vision and a reality in poetry pure and simple which make them, if not mysterious, at least marvellous. As with some phrase of Mozart or Beethoven one might say: 'How simple, a child could do it; besides which, a child can and does thoroughly enjoy it:—yet is it not very difficult, almost impossible, to conceive such a simple phrase?' So these children's poems have no grand upholstery to smother them or, to return to music, they are not drowned in complications of orchestra and scoring.

They are as tiny as a grasshopper's little thin treble in the grass, yet each one is so perfect that whoever reads it must exclaim over it, 'Oh, if I could have written that! It is so simple that it looks easy and yet I believe it would be easier to write one of Keats' Odes, or even Milton's than one of these'. A few extracts will illustrate my meaning:

Hope is like a harebell trembling from its birth,
Love is like a rose the joy of all the earth;
Faith is like a lily lifted high and white,
Love is like a lovely rose the world's delight;
Harebells and sweet lilies show a thornless growth,
But the rose with all its thorns excels them both.

O wind, why do you never rest,
  Wandering, whistling to and fro,
Bringing rain out of the west,
  From the dim north bringing snow?

'I dreamt I caught a little owl
And the bird was blue—'

'But you may hunt for ever
And not find such an one.'

'I dreamt I set a sunflower,
And red as blood it grew—'

'But such a sunflower never
Bloomed beneath the sun.'

On the grassy banks
Lambkins at their pranks;
Woolly sisters, woolly brothers,
    Jumping off their feet,
While their woolly mothers
    Watch by them and bleat.

The dear old woman in the lane
    Is sick and sore with pains and aches,
We'll go to her this afternoon,
    And take her tea and eggs and cakes.

We'll stop to make the kettle boil,
    And brew some tea, and set the tray,
And poach an egg, and toast a cake,
    And wheel her chair round, if we may.

Brownie, Brownie, let down your milk,
White as swansdown and smooth as silk,
Fresh as dew and pure as snow:
For I know where the cowslips blow,
And you shall have a cowslip wreath
No sweeter scented than your breath.

Growing in the vale
    By the uplands hilly,
Growing straight and frail,
    Lady Daffadowndilly.

In a golden crown,
And a scant green gown
    While the spring blows chilly,
Lady Daffadown,
    Sweet Daffadowndilly.

Rushes in a watery place,
   And reeds in a hollow;
A soaring skylark in the sky,
   A darting swallow;
And where pale blossom used to hang
   Ripe fruit to follow.

    Minnie and Mattie
      And fat little May,
    Out in the country,
      Spending a day.

    Such a bright day,
      With the sun glowing,
    And the trees half in leaf,
      And the grass growing....

Heartsease in my garden bed,
   With sweetwilliam white and red,
Honeysuckle on my wall:—
   Heartsease blossoms in my heart
When sweet William comes to call;
   But it withers when we part,
And the honey-trumpets fall.

O sailor, come ashore,
   What have you brought for me?
Red coral, white coral,
   Coral from the sea.

I did not dig it from the ground,
   Nor pluck it from a tree;
Feeble insects made it
   In the stormy sea.

Who has seen the wind?
  Neither I nor you:
But when the leaves hang trembling
  The wind is passing thro'.

Who has seen the wind?
  Neither you nor I:
But when the trees bow down their heads
  The wind is passing by.

An emerald is as green as grass;
  A ruby red as blood;
A sapphire shines as blue as heaven;
  A flint lies in the mud.

A diamond is a brilliant stone,
  To catch the world's desire;
An opal holds a fiery spark;
  But a flint holds fire.

Blind from my birth,
Where flowers are springing
I sit on earth
All dark.
Hark! Hark!
A lark is singing,
His notes are all for me,
For me his mirth:—
Till some day I shall see
Beautiful flowers
And birds in bowers
Where all joy-bells are ringing.

Some will be reminded of Blake in reading these
poems. They have not the weight of symbolical

sorrow that drops from the wings of the *Songs of Innocence*, causing the cries of the birds and lambs and babies to be more awful than words of judgment or doom, so piercing is the poet's pity for the wrongs of tiny children and all God's innocent creatures. Christina Rossetti was like Blake in her love and veneration for innocence—children, lambs, birds, dogs, cats, rabbits, bees, caterpillars, flowers and sea beasts—but in *Sing Song* she is telling children about these creatures, showing their innocence, their gaiety, their meekness, their drollery, fun and jollity, without relation to the cruel facts of life that surround them. Yet, even if we take *Sing Song* as being what it is, merely a collection of short poems for children, full of intimate vision, fancy and fun, there is in each of them that drop of distilling genius which makes of their very drollery and innocence something, not indeed as in Blake's 'Chimney Sweep's Song' marrow-dissolving and haunting, but something so charged with the unconscious pathos which is the soul of childhood itself that it leaves one with the sense of sadness mingling in the sunbeams and the taste of tears in all the honey. A great deal has been said about the sadness of Christina Rossetti's devotional poems, about the morbidity of her mind as expressed in these and others which reveal conflict and the actual struggles that went on in her

personal life. To my mind, the whole sadness together
with the final sweet and satisfying firmness of faith
and cheerfulness of the woman seem most noble,
because most unconscious, in these childlike but
never childish verses. In the little poem about
poaching an egg for the old woman's tea, in the
friendly one that extols a piece of coal by contrast
with jewels, in that which gives the essence of the
wind passing to and fro, in the fateful and again
Blake-like dream of the blue owl and the blood-red
sunflower, one sees the same broad benignant recognition of the prerogative of all things daily and
accustomed to become in their turn things un-
accustomed and unfrequent and rarely, deeply, significant. With one blow, as it were, she strikes
at the very root of a problem in aesthetics and kills
off a number of foolish or at least superficial defini-
tions about what poetry, rightly speaking, ought or
ought not to be.

It will be seen by reading all her work that she
wrote so easily and had so pure and natural a diction
that some of her 'grown-up' poems are almost as
simple as those which were written for children.

On the wind of January
    Down flits the snow,
Travelling from the frozen North
    As cold as it can blow.

> Poor robin redbreast,
>   Look where he comes;
> Let him in to feel your fire,
>   And toss him of your crumbs.

So begins 'A Year's Windfalls'.

Then there must be mentioned a special quality of hers, noticeable in a latent sense in the 'Pageant', more obvious in *Sing Song*—namely, her humour. It is a thread of gold in all the homely warp of her letters. It is seldom, one feels, at all absent from her mood even when she writes with melancholy, although it is difficult to explain how one feels this humorousness, which must not be confused with the occasional flash of irony she sometimes showed.

> My blindest buzzard that I know,
>   My special mole, when will you see?
>   Oh no, you must not look at me,
> There's nothing hid for me to show.

But in this little book, which does not pretend to be an adequate study of Christina Rossetti's *whole* work, I must not be tempted to stray from the root to the branches when these again branch out and become twigs. The root, the main stem of this genius, is God-loving, beauty-loving, spiritualised, earth-loving *observation*: the same translated on the one side into vivid, glowing colours and on the other into instant, spontaneous music—I had almost written bird-song, for the notes are so natural; they are like Shakespeare's 'wood notes wild' and bring no echo of the academy.

We may take as an example of this freshness of observation almost any of her lyrics, good or indifferent. All bear the print of careless power where description of natural beauties is concerned and all the glow of the author's vivid love of water, of grass, trees, flowers and fruit.

For fruit and its blossom she had a deep craving admiration. Set beside the glories of the goblin fruit 'An Apple gathering' with its tribute to blossoms in the opening lines:

> I plucked pink blossoms from mine apple-tree
> And wore them all that evening in my hair.

Set beside this 'A Birthday' which, like 'When I am dead, my dearest', is a favourite poem of hers, well-known to anthology readers, that must be quoted whole or not at all:

> My heart is like a singing bird
> Whose nest is in a watered shoot:
> My heart is like an apple-tree
> Whose boughs are bent with thickset fruit;
> My heart is like a rainbow shell
> That paddles in a halcyon sea;
> My heart is gladder than all these
> Because my love is come to me.

Raise me a dais of silk and down;
  Hang it with vair and purple dyes;
Carve it in doves and pomegranates,
  And peacocks with a hundred eyes;
Work it in gold and silver grapes,
  In leaves and silver fleurs-de-lys;
Because the birthday of my life
  Is come, my love is come to me.

This picture brings before us the Pre-Raphaelite accessories, the gorgeous colours and mysterious embroideries—the created atmosphere being one of half-sensuous, half-mystic and wholly poetic beauty. But there the likeness to the prevalent temper of those young painters ceases; for, by its simplicity in music and perfect naturalness and spontaneity of the emotions, the poem belongs clearly to Christina and bears her special mark as much as 'Winter Rain' does, work of the same period but of the most realistic and straightforward pattern.

Every valley drinks,
  Every dell and hollow;
Where the kind rain sinks and sinks,
  Green of Spring will follow.

Yet a lapse of weeks—
  Buds will burst their edges,
Strip their wool-coats, glue-coats, streaks,
  In the woods and hedges....

In a long poem dated 1865 called 'The Iniquity of the Fathers upon the Children', a poem which

is slightly reminiscent of both Tennyson and Mrs
Browning, she gives us a little dreary etching which
is admirable in its neat detachment:

> Our one-street village stood
> A long mile from the town,
> A mile of windy down
> And bleak one-sided wood,
> With not a single house.
> Our town itself was small,
> With just the common shops,
> And throve in its small way.

It forms a good opening for the tragic story which
follows.

This realism of Christina Rossetti's is spasmodic
only, her mystical, dreamy soul was never long content
to be entirely busy with what she could see or touch.

In some of the longer narrative poems such as
'Prince's Progress', we have examples of realism in
the treatment of nature blended with highly de-
corative accessories like those in 'A Birthday' and
'Apple-Gathering' and others. In yet a third class
of poem she describes a background whilst telling an
allegorical story which has the passionate and interior quality of a religious picture, rapt and remote.
'From House to Home' provides a striking example
of this type. It is a long and fervent narrative,
allegorical in character, very intense, tuned to a
certain interior key of meditative spirituality and

tainted ever so slightly by feverishness of vision. It tells of a succession of states of being, dream-like in character. In the first of these the teller of the story is living in a kind of Earthly Paradise and is surrounded by trees, and animals of all kinds. (Notice the way in which Christina Rossetti's fondness for all animals, birds and insects never deserts her in any scheme of a perfectly pictured universe.) Here the meadows, lawns, trees and flowers are as much displayed for the benefit of squirrels, birds and beasts as they are meant to regale the happy dreamer. There is a somewhat detailed description of the beauteous 'pleasure-place':

My castle stood of white transparent glass
   Glittering and frail with many a fretted spire,
But when the summer sunset came to pass
   It kindled into fire.

My pleasaunce was an undulating green,
   Stately with trees whose shadows slept below,
With glimpses of smooth garden-beds between
   Like flame or sky or snow.

Swift squirrels on the pastures took their ease,
   With leaping lambs safe from the unfeared knife;
All singing-birds rejoicing in those trees
   Fulfilled their careless life.

Woodpigeons cooed there, stockdoves nestled there;
   My trees were full of songs and flowers and fruit;
Their branches spread a city to the air
   And mice lodged in their root.

*   *   *   *

Frogs and fat toads were there to hop or plod
   And propagate in peace, an uncouth crew,
Where velvet-headed rushes rustling nod
   And spill the morning dew.

But she is called away by one 'like an angel'
who 'oft-times walked with me', one with 'spirit-
discerning eyes' who bids her leave her pleasaunce
and her happy dream to follow him. Day and
night she seeks for him, but he has vanished.
'My heart broke', cries the dreamer, and then she
hears a voice from among many voices of spirits
saying, 'She hath suffered long', and another voice
answers, 'Make her see'. What she sees is a marvellously beautiful woman who is chained to the
heavens.

Her eyes were like some fire-enshrining gem....
   She stood on inner ground that budded flowers....
But every flower was lifted on a thorn,
   And every thorn shot upright from its sands
To gall her feet; hoarse laughter pealed in scorn
   With cruel clapping hands.

"One cried, 'How long?'"—she is given a cup of gall
to drink, but a ministering hand distils into it 'wine
and virgin honey'.

Her lips and cheeks waxed rosy-fresh and young;
   Drinking she sang 'My soul shall nothing want';
And drank anew: while soft a song was sung,
   A mystical slow chant.

       *   *   *   *

Then earth and heaven were rolled up like a scroll;
  Time and space, change and death, had passed
      away;
Weight, number, measure, each had reached its
      whole:
  The day had come, that day.

Multitudes—multitudes—stood up in bliss,
  Made equal to the angels, glorious, fair;
With harps, palms, wedding-garments, kiss of
      peace,
  And crowned and haloed hair.

That the martyred woman in this poem is meant in
some sense to be the Christian Church; the narrator,
the poetess herself; and the 'pleasure-place' in which
the story begins, her ideal of fair and happy life
which for so many reasons had to be relinquished,
there is small room for doubt.

'Repining' is another poem belonging to this
group, all of the bodeful, dreamy, interior type which
still keeps narrative form. In it and in 'An Old-
World Thicket' there is the same complaining note,
the same minor sadness of key, while nature in each
of these poems actually lends her comely counten-
ance and willing accessories to aid the spiritual
strangeness and intense sorrowfulness of the inner
drama that is being enacted.

  The nightingale since set of sun
  Her throbbing music had not done.

What potency and urgent expectancy there are in
these words from 'Repining'. In 'An Old-World
Thicket' there is still more strangeness, and through
it all how sweetly her love of water and bird-song
prevails:

Awake or sleeping (for I know not which)
  I was or was not mazed within a wood
  Where every mother-bird brought up her brood
    Safe in some leafy niche
Of oak or ash, of cypress or of beech,

Of silvery aspen trembling delicately,
  Of plane or warmer-tinted sycomore,
  Of elm that dies in secret from the core,
    Of ivy weak and free,
Of pines, of all green lofty things that be.

    *   *   *   *

A sound of waters neither rose nor sank,
  And spread a sense of freshness through the air;
  It seemed not here or there, but everywhere,
    As if the whole earth drank,
Root fathom-deep and strawberry on its bank.

    *   *   *   *

Without my will I hearkened and I heard
  (Asleep or waking, for I know not which),
  Till note by note the music changed its pitch;
    Bird ceased to answer bird,
And every wind sighed softly if it stirred.

The drip of widening waters seemed to weep,
  All fountains sobbed and gurgled as they sprang,
Somewhere a cataract cried out in its leap
    Sheer down a headlong steep;
  High over all cloud-thunders gave a clang.

Of water, indeed, she was deeply, mystically fond.
She constantly mentions it in her poems:

> My heart is like a singing bird
>   Whose nest is in a watered shoot.
>
> ('A Birthday', 1857.)

> Every valley drinks,
>   Every dell and hollow;
> Where the kind rain sinks and sinks,
>   Green of Spring will follow.
>
> ('Winter Rain', 1859.)

> All earth's full rivers cannot fill
> The sea, that drinking thirsteth still.
>
> ('By the Sea', 1858.)

> There are rivers lapsing down
>   Lily-laden to the sea.
>
> ('By the Water', 1856.)

> A bubbling streamlet flowed o'er sand
> Pebbly and fine, and sent life up
> Green succous stalk and flower-cup.
>
> ('Repining', 1847.)

She loved the places where water flowed, with
tears she was friendly, pleased with showers and
fountains, joyous with the sea. She learned much
from the climate of England: it gave her her heavenly
dews, her mists and her sweet wholesome moisture.

As one reads her poetry, this mystical fondness

for water is an ever-increasingly dominant feature in the soul landscape which she presents.

> 'Sweet Life is dead.'—'Not so:
> I meet him day by day,
> Where bluest fountains flow
> And trees are white as snow,
> For it is time of May.'

In these lines from the lyric 'May' we cannot but note the symbolic use of the fountain. Where there is water, there is life—where there is water, there is the means of regeneration.

At other times she seems to seek water and fire together—complementary elements both signifying the purification of the soul:

> I seek the sea of glass and fire
> To wash the spot, to burn the snare.[1]

'To *wash* the spot', that is the key-note of much of her religious verse and sums up her feeling of love for water, the sea, sorrow and grace.

Dreams are frequently the medium of her verse. In 'An Old-World Thicket', that strange tapestry of words, where the leaves and the butterflies, the waters and the flowers, seem to belong to the tranced world of 'Kubla Khan', of the 'Sensitive Plant' or

---

[1] From 'The Convent Threshold', a most important poem among those which illustrate Christina Rossetti's penitential and sacramental leanings.

of the pictures of Dante Rossetti—the setting is a dream. 'Birds of Paradise' is another half-mystical poem and here, while there is no fountain or river, there is music at its most melodious and a glory of light that is, I believe, unparalleled in any of her other poems. Something in its exquisite beauty is akin to the work of Dante Gabriel Rossetti.

Golden-winged, silver-winged,
　　Winged with flashing flame,
Such a flight of birds I saw,
　　Birds without a name:
Singing songs in their own tongue—
　　Song of songs—they came.

One to another calling,
　　Each answering each,
One to another calling
In their proper speech:
High above my head they wheeled,
　　Far out of reach.

On wings of flame they went and came
　　With a cadenced clang:
　　Their silver wings tinkled,
　　Their golden wings rang;
The wind it whistled through their wings
　　Where in heaven they sang.

They flashed and they darted
　　Awhile before mine eyes,
Mounting, mounting, mounting still,
　　In haste to scale the skies,
Birds without a nest on earth,
　　Birds of Paradise.

Birds, sheep and lambs, roses, the sea and fresh
water, dreams and the places where water makes
dreams flower, sunlight, moonlight and starlight.
These are some of the oftenest recurring themes in
her poetry, whether sacred or secular. The seasons
pre-occupied her, and whichever one she chose to
celebrate seems at the moment to have held her
heart's peculiar devotion. No one has ever com-
memorated the very perfume of flowers as she did.
Summer was a season she loved dearly, and in the
London of the Rossettis' day was still appreciable,
not only in the city parks, but in the old bird-
haunted gardens such as the famous one at 16
Cheyne Walk, where Dante Gabriel Rossetti kept
his wombat and his other familiar pets. Doubtless
there were nestlings in the roof at Torrington Square;
doubtless Christina, frail and suffering through the
fogs and frosts of winter and early spring, had full
and enough cause to write the lines:

> May is scant and crude,
> Generous June is riper.

'Generous June', how beautiful that is.

But we could understand little of Christina Rossetti's mind unless we were prepared to recognise
that the mainspring of its beauty, the core in all
this living growth, colour and radiance of song was
her love of God. Whether she writes directly or

indirectly of that love, we feel it; we feel it to be the
sun whose light and heat have nourished all her
blossoms, whether they be things of exquisite design
and fancy, like 'Goblin Market', 'A Birthday',
'Birds of Paradise' or 'Maiden Song', or whether
they be songs sad and drooping in character such as
the one in her prose tale *Maude* beginning 'Fade,
tender lily', or whether again they be in some measure
directly inspired by religious thoughts and feelings
such as those which filled her devotional books.

I will take one example of these last (from 'Some
Feasts and Fasts') which does most perfectly blend
the two colours in consciousness of which I am
speaking, the love of God and love of the beauty of
God's creation:

WHITSUN EVE

The white dove cooeth in her downy nest,
Keeping her young ones warm beneath her breast:
The white moon saileth through the cool clear sky,
Screened by a tender mist in passing by:
The white rose buds, with thorns upon its stem,
All the more precious and more dear for them:
The stream shines silver in the tufted grass,
The white clouds scarcely dim it as they pass;
Deep in the valleys lily cups are white,
They send up incense all the holy night.
Our souls are white, made clean in Blood once shed:
White blessed Angels watch around our bed:—
O spotless Lamb of God, still keep us so,
Thou who wert born for us in time of snow.

Here all that is purest in nature is pressed into the service of the one shining and immaculate lamb, dove, soul and source of divinely created things. The effect is somewhat that of a picture by Botticelli representing angels and lilies with gold and silver trumpets, with hills where the flocks feed, silvered by sun and moon together and, in the foreground, the luxuriance of exquisite petals, while the whole is breathed on by some light and glowing colour more like a perfume than any known hue. Indeed, many of the verses written to celebrate feasts and fasts somehow, to my mind, always recall paintings of the early Italian masters so beloved of all the Rossetti family. Nothing is vague and nebulous about Christina Rossetti's imagination and, as in the delicious poem called 'Child's talk in April', so with these devotional pictures of hers all is gem-clear and water-bright—her skies are felt to be deeply blue, her doves and lambs snowy. Her feasts are real feasts regaling the senses with brightness and perfume, and her fasts true fasts or vigils tasting of the sands of Arabia and bitter with the salt of human tears.

Ash Wednesday

My God, My God, have mercy on my sin,
For it is great; and if I should begin
To tell it all, the day would be too small
    To tell it in.

My God, Thou wilt have mercy on my sin
For Thy Love's sake: yea, if I should begin
To tell This all, the day would be too small
    To tell it in.

Hardly a change is here to be perceived in tone, in touch, or in deep, indwelling emotion when we open George Herbert's poems and read these lines from the one called 'Discipline':

    For my heart's desire
    Unto Thine is bent:
      I aspire
    To a full consent,

and later,

    Though I fail, I weep;
    Though I halt in pace,
      Yet I creep
    To the throne of grace.

Another poem among those which celebrate feasts or fasts and which gives us an exquisite glimpse of Christina Rossetti in her inmost womanliness of soul is this on Christmastide:

    Love came down at Christmas,
      Love all lovely, Love Divine;
    Love was born at Christmas,
      Star and Angels gave the sign.

    Worship we the Godhead,
      Love Incarnate, Love Divine;
    Worship we our Jesus:
      But wherewith for sacred sign?

> Love shall be our token,
> Love be yours and love be mine,
> Love to God and all men,
> Love for plea and gift and sign.

In 'Christmas Day' she speaks of our Lord as the 'flower of babies'. Surely Saint Francis and, in a later day, the Little Flower Saint Teresa of the Child Jesus could not have invented anything sweeter, and would have smiled on this artless and heavenly-minded conception:

> Lily of lilies He
> Upon His Mother's knee;
> Rose of roses, soon to be
> Crowned with thorns on leafless tree.

That is more tender than anything of the same kind that I know unless it be 'The Burning Babe' by Father Southwell.

But just as Christina Rossetti had variety of moods and modes of expression in her secular, so in her devotional work she was various. All the devotional poems bear her mark. They are, as it were, a flock, easily recognisable by something at once simple (she never searched for the uncommon word although it sometimes came, she searched for and generally found the right word), direct, intense in feeling, unaffected; feminine in being so direct, so untrammelled by tiresome ponderous learning, always reverent, self-forgetting. There are, indeed,

occasionally monotonies in her religious verse, and
these could sometimes becloud her other work. They
came, perhaps, from the weakness of her body;
anaemia sometimes tinges her work with a tragic
suggestion of what might have been, and there is a
rare, but very rare, tendency to fall into the commonplace of poetic idea. But it is still astonishing
to notice in how many ways Christina Rossetti could
and did approach her central religious theme of the
love of God. She could write peacefully, and she
could, as we have seen, paint some exquisite pictures
of one of the sublime things in religion—the birth of
our Lord, or the celebration of some Church feast
carried out in the natural sphere. The saints, apostles
and early Church martyrs inspired her, and she could
write of angels with the inspiration of a soul that has
known something of the true ecstasy of prayer and
vision. Nevertheless, she could and did often write
that poignant and most awful thing, a poem of the
soul's own inmost drama; its fears, its penitence, its
hopes, its anguish, dryness and desolation, all cry
aloud in turn in these molten outpourings of hers.
In a single year she wrote two such tragic heart-
cries which show most clearly that, for all her gentle
joyousness in natural things, Christina Rossetti's
peace of mind was not cheaply bought and her
religious life was, especially in youth, one long in-

terior struggle towards harmony, one unceasing and relentlessly exhausting fight against self. The names of these two poems are 'A Better Resurrection' and 'The Heart knows its own Bitterness'. Of this last the opening stanza is most intense:

> When all the over-work of life
>   Is finished once, and fast asleep
> We swerve no more beneath the knife
>   But taste that silence cool and deep;
> Forgetful of the highways rough,
>   Forgetful of the thorny scourge,
>   Forgetful of the tossing surge,
> Then shall we find it is enough?

And later on in the same poem she says:

> I used to labour, used to strive
>   For pleasure with a restless will:
> Now if I save my soul alive
>   All else what matters, good or ill?

And then later on showing something of the sincere but fierce ardours of a young Saint Teresa:

> You scratch my surface with your pin,
>   You stroke me smooth with hushing breath:—
> Nay pierce, nay probe, nay dig within,
>   Probe my quick core and sound my depth.
> You call me with a puny call,
>   You talk, you smile, you nothing do:
>   How should I spend my heart on you,
> My heart that so outweighs you all?

Christina Rossetti was twenty-seven when she wrote this, and it has a note of noble impatience and young intensity and ardour that are winning in their humanity. On her, small-talk, quiet sociable parties, the interchange of nothings which are the current coin of society, sometimes grated; one sees that in her prose tale *Maude*—for Maude was evidently in some sense a portrait of the author, and Maude is proud, and Maude has a deep passionate soul that rebels against the trivial round of tea parties and domestic duties; nevertheless, Maude's punishment, a wearisome illness and an early death, is an indication of what her youthful creator thought to be the fitting deserts of too much vehemence and too great spiritual pride. Of spiritual pride Christina Rossetti can have known really very little, her vehemence was scarcely apparent in life. It may almost have come as a surprise to those who knew her in her unassuming everyday rôle of daughter, sister, housekeeper, even in her gentle aspect of artistry, to read the fiery verses I have just quoted. But none of her admirers can have been surprised at the close of her poem:

> Eye hath not seen nor ear hath heard
> > Nor heart conceived that full 'enough':
> Here moans the separating sea,
> > Here harvests fail, here breaks the heart:
> > There God shall join and no man part,
> I full of Christ and Christ of me.

This was the noble and perfect harmony towards

which she strove, and this the goal of all her ambition. It was as though all the windows in her soul's house faced the east and these windows were always wide open to meet the glory of an ever-instreaming eternal sunrise:

> Oh my soul, she beats her wings
>   And pants to fly away
> Up to immortal things
>   In the heavenly day:
> Yet she flags and almost faints:
>   Can such be meant for me?—
> 'Come and see,' say the Saints;
>   Saith Jesus: 'Come and see'.

'I will lift up mine eyes unto the hills', the poem from which I have just quoted, is one of those in which love and triumph seem to beat down the rising despair.

Again in 'How long?' the inspiration of vision perfectly achieves its glowing purpose and is spiritualised by the framework of a verse:

> Give me an Angel's heart, that day nor night
> Rests not from adoration its delight,
> Still crying 'Holy holy' in the height.

An 'Angel's heart'—it is a wonderful image; Blake alone or Crashaw could have achieved such mysterious simplicity.

One can well believe that her true life was attuned to things of spiritual wonder and that she passed

much of her time, whether awake or dreaming, in
the garden whose tenants are those birds

> Golden-winged, silver-winged,
> Winged with flashing flame,

described in her poem 'Birds of Paradise':

> Not in any garden
> That mortal foot hath trod,
> Not in any flowering tree
> That springs from earthly sod,
> But in the garden where they dwell,
> The Paradise of God.

On this Paradise she constantly pondered. Her soul
was very easily unmoored from its few earthly tram-
mels. In spite of the inner conflict that engaged her
frequent attention, in spite of all life's inescapable
dreariness, of pain and the anguish which her
sensitive nerves underwent, yet her devotional
poems are quite as often poems of ecstasy and praise,
of artistic delight in the loveliness of her heavenly
vision and thankfulness for the beauty of earth-
innocent as they are poems of desolation, of the sense
of God's righteous wrath and of the fear and oppres-
sions of earth-guilty. The truth is that her genius
was essentially a thing of light, of brilliant, lambent
warmth and sweetness. She was most truly herself
when she was happy, and the accounts given by her
biographers of the happiness and brightness of her
early youth and childhood seem to show that

Christina Rossetti was, to borrow from the language of children, 'meant to be happy'.

She had the sensitiveness to all impressions of an artist. This, together with her highly scrupulous conscience (which was constantly binding her to make difficult and painful renouncements), was to a great extent the cause of melancholy and bitterness of heart with which she was sometimes afflicted. Her poems have been called morbid because in some of them she reveals this other side of the picture, a shadowy and sensitive shrinking of the soul, a *recueillement*, so to speak, and a sense of the pain and the frequent flatness of life. But these tendencies should not be deplored as they have been. There was never anything unwholesome or indeed unnatural in Christina Rossetti's sadness. Given Christina Rossetti, and given the world with its ruthlessness, its mystery of pain and innocent suffering, its mysteries of sin and of the Fall, how could it have been otherwise? In her there was never any seeking after sorrow for sorrow's own sake, much less any morbid pandering to egotistical self-analysis. Her penitence was a thing like her joy, childlike and noble, all her response was generous and self-forgetting. That she was lonely in her very beauty of soul was but the price she had to pay for being a poet at all, and in a marvellous manner this loneliness of spirit did spring from her love of God—love of God being, as I mean to try to show, the heart-pulse and mainspring of her whole poetic output.

In Christina Rossetti this love is seen always or almost always under one aspect; for her God was oftener thought of in the glorious second Person of the Trinity than in either the first or the third. She was like George Herbert in her conversations with her Lord, and like the holy anchoress of Norwich, the Lady Juliana, in her deep sense of the marvel of the redemption. Our blessed Lord's Passion, His agony on the Cross, were her constant pre-occupations and it is not too much to say that her religious life was indeed rooted on Calvary. She was, as I have said before, extremely scrupulous and inclining towards self-accusation, thus her poems have a constantly recurring straining note of repentance. She stood, as it were, on the lowest step of the altar in the house of God's poetry:

Mea culpa, mea culpa, mea maxima culpa

was the burden of her every heart beat:

O Lord, my heart is broken for my sin:
Yet hasten Thine own day
And come away.
Is not time full? Oh put the sickle in,
O Lord, begin!

So ends "Ye have forgotten the Exhortation".

Another clear example of the loving and penitential notes blending together is a little poem called
'For under a Crucifix'.

> Once I ached for thy dear sake;
> Wilt thou cause Me now to ache?
> Once I bled for thee in pain;
> Wilt thou pierce My Heart again?
>
> Crown of thorns and shameful tree,
> Bitter death I bore for thee,
> Gave up glory, broke My will,—
> And canst thou reject Me still?

On the whole, the variety of these devotional
poems strikes one more and more as one reads and
re-reads them. She had a perfect touch for a religious theme and could be almost gay, as in the
beautiful 'Christmas Day' beginning

> A baby is a harmless thing.

Or she could be broadly and nobly expansive, filling
out her metre and contracting it again to suit a theme
of speculative or imaginative breadth of vision. She
could write something sharp and poignant such as
the well-known

> Does the road wind up-hill all the way?
>   Yes, to the very end.
> Will the day's journey take the whole long day?
>   From morn to night, my friend.

With its quietly perfect closing lines about the inn
where the tired traveller is to rest at last:

> Will there be beds for me and all who seek?
>   Yea, beds for all who come.

And she could paint a picture of exquisite peace as
in 'The Watchers':

> She fell asleep among the flowers
> In the sober autumn hours.

She could celebrate the varying feasts and fasts of
the Church with most lovely and appropriate words.
It was as if her mind was a garden whose very soil
was that in which the seeds of grace could flower and
spring easily. Watered with tears, enriched with
much suffering, costing much effort, it brought forth
flowers homely and heavenly alike. From it nothing
cheerful was banished, heartsease, campanula nor
wallflower; rose and peony blushed there; but in it
there were many lilies, things holding special and
secret light, tall delicate blooms of Solomon's seal
secreting its pearls beneath the broad green banners,
grasses and wild delicate tendrils; nooks for rabbit,
mole and moorhen: water and water-lilies and
'haunts of coot and hern'. But the rarest of all her
mind's symbolic flowers was its passion-flower—its
love of God.

Various as are the strands in the warp and woof of Christina Rossetti's poems, I have so far endeavoured to deal somewhat at length with the two main currents of her thought, the imaginative and the devotional. There are, of course, some poems streaked and pied like violets or pansies, the blue of heaven mingling with the brown or the green of earth, the golden alchemy of heavenly vision touching into relief the violets and damsons of some darker reverie.

And then there are the children's poems, *Sing Song*, but as most of these attain to a very high level of artistic achievement and are indeed some of her most beautiful work, I have included them in my remarks on her secular poems at the beginning of this chapter.

It is now time to pass on to the prose works, but before I do this I must quote from one or two of her light or definitely humorous poems, for she had a great featness in composing a fable or in limning a portrait, and examples of these arts of hers should not be wanting in any serious attempt to appreciate the scope of her talent. I quote first from ' Portraits '

An easy lazy length of limb,
  Dark eyes and features from the South,
A short-legged meditative pipe
  Set in a supercilious mouth:

Ink and a pen and papers laid
  Down on a table for the night,
Beside a semi-dozing man
  Who wakes to go to bed by light.

* * * *

A pair of brothers brotherly,
  Unlike and yet how much the same
In heart and high-toned intellect,
  In face and bearing, hope and aim:
Friends of the self-same treasured friends
  And of one home the dear delight,
Beloved of many a loving heart,
  And cherished both in mine, Good-night.

Then there is this, less serious but successful in its
likeness:

The P.R.B. is in its decadence:
  For Woolner in Australia cooks his chops,
  And Hunt is yearning for the land of Cheops;
    D. G. Rossetti shuns the vulgar optic;
  While William M. Rossetti merely lops
    His B's in English disesteemed as Coptic;
  Calm Stephens in the twilight smokes his pipe,
    But long the dawning of his public day;
    And he at last the champion great Millais,
  Attaining academic opulence,
    Winds up his signature with A.R.A.
So rivers merge in the perpetual sea;
So luscious fruit must fall when over-ripe;
And so the consummated P.R.B.

In 'Child's Talk in April' there is humour blended

with quaint powers of observation and much charm;
it begins:

> I wish you were a pleasant wren,
>   And I your small accepted mate;
> How we'd look down on toilsome men!
>   We'd rise and go to bed at eight
>   Or it may be not quite so late

and the description of the hatching out of the nestlings is delightful—'Fancy the breaking of the shell'
and then:

> Fancy the embryo coats of down,
>   The gradual feathers soft and sleek.

In one much longer poem, called 'Freaks of
Fashion', she matches humour with real flashes of
wit and attains to an extraordinarily high level in
this kind of light verse. It is a fable in the style of
La Fontaine where all the birds get together in the
early spring to discuss what the fashions are going
to be. The birds' characters are marvellously drawn
and the whole dialogue is delicious in its drollery;
the range of vocabulary being startlingly good.
I quote some of the verses:

> Robin says: 'A scarlet waistcoat
>   Will be all the wear,
> Snug, and also cheerful-looking
>   For the frostiest air,
> Comfortable for the chest too
>   When one comes to plume and pair'.

'Neat grey hoods will be in vogue',
   Quoth a Jackdaw: 'glossy grey,
Setting close, yet setting easy,
   Nothing fly-away;
Suited to our misty mornings,
   À la négligée.'

Flushing salmon, flushing sulphur,
   Haughty Cockatoos
Answer—'Hoods may do for mornings,
   But for evenings choose
High head-dresses, curved like crescents
   Such as well-bred persons use'.

And then, after four more delightful stanzas,

Then a Stork took up the word:
   'Aim at height and *chic*:
Not high heels, they're common; somehow,
   Stilted legs, not thick,
Nor yet thin': he just glanced downward
   And snapped-to his beak.

That stork is a masterpiece. Do we not all know him—or her?

Chapter Three

HER PROSE

To us Christians the land of the shadow of death is no longer the dominion of the king of terrors, but rather a tiring-closet for the bride of the King of kings.

(Seek and Find, p. 150)

In this chapter I am going to try to say something about Christina Rossetti's considerable gifts as a prose writer. She was, it will be conceded by anyone who has studied her longer devotional commentaries such as *The Face of the Deep*, a commentary on the Apocalypse, capable of writing very grandly and very simply at once, and altogether in a manner well suited to the sublime themes which she chose. In *Time Flies*, a reading diary, she writes in more homely fashion and tells delightful little anecdotes of animals, plants and foreign peoples, thus pointing the morals which she expounds. Each day is given its share of verse or story, and when that day has a saint (and that most days have one Christina Rossetti was sure) she gives the biography of the saint in terse and quiet English. *Called to be Saints* is another diary of the same kind, but more fanciful in its arrangement. *Seek and Find* is a very beautiful little accompaniment to the *Benedicite*. But good as is the prose in all these works, how splendid are the flashes of real poetry when they come, how refreshing and how truly is poetry the writer's own best medium of self-expression. Indeed, the boldness and freedom of spirit which characterised Christina Rossetti's verse did not always show in her prose. Her letters are singularly bare of any poetical or picturesque motive and although she describes accurately and sometimes beautifully the plants and jewels which she assigns to each of her saints in *Called to be Saints*, it has just occasionally struck me that the real Christina Rossetti was not entirely at ease in this medium—she needed metre as well as thought, music as well as colour, to clothe and give wings to her spirit. Whether it was that her rigorous self-discipline in daily life sometimes hampered and impeded her imagination, or whether it was that she did not care to unloosen her entire mind in such writings, the fact remains that, viewed as a prose writer, she is interesting, distinguished, but far less significant than she is when viewed as a poet. Her letters and her other prose works are not, like Dorothy Wordsworth's Journal, the intimate record of a personality. In Dorothy Wordsworth's Journal we find the raw material of what afterwards became her brother's poetry. But the raw material is itself poetic in intensity and beautifully fresh. She could describe a scene or a wayside meeting; she could convey the very essence of a day in spring or autumn until the wind, the scents of the spring flowers, the wild cries of birds, and their movements and rustlings, their shadowings amid bare branches or thick foliage are felt upon the pages.

Turn to any one of Christina Rossetti's exquisite nature poems and there is the same buoyancy of freedom and at-homeness with birds or blossoms, bees, flowers, cows and streams, coming at her bidding or departing to make room for the snowflake or the shivering autumnal scene at her nod. There are no passages quite like these in her prose works. In them she is so much more conscious, heavier and more constrained than when writing poetry. They suggest somehow to me a careful pruning, almost a self-distrust—the artist is now waiting in humble attendance upon the student of self-discipline and the disciple in the house of pain.

The Face of the Deep is rich in noble litanies and exquisite verses, in wise and gentle precept. But somehow (I submit this opinion with great self-distrust, and offer it merely as a personal and therefore unimportant piece of criticism) I feel it to be a little over-elaborate. The Book of Revelation is surely too astounding in its other-worldly simplicity, its sheer realism of the spirit, to be studied in this

literal manner. Nevertheless, for those who have a
mind to read slowly with digestion in quiet and
reflective moments, this long commentary, with its
tender upshooting of verse and its grave and penitential tone, will yield many glories for inspection.
How beautiful, for example, are these words

A holy grave is the true bed of heartsease. And
already the flowers appear on the earth although
the winter is not yet past.

They have the flavour, or rather one should say the
perfume, of Sir Thomas Browne. At other times she
seems to echo some of the old Anglican divines and
theologians of the seventeenth century with their
sense of noble rhythmic prose; in prayer she is their
child:—

'O Lord Jesus,' she writes, 'my Lord Jesus, Thou
art Light to our darkness, Knowledge for our ignorance, Wisdom for our folly, Certainty for our doubts.
Thou art our Way and our End; the Illumination of
our way, the Glory of our end. Never shall we see,
know, have, enjoy, aught permanent out of Thee;
but in Thee (please God!) all: for whoso is one with
Thee cannot but see with Thine Eyes, acquiesce in
Thy Will, apprehend by Thine Understanding,
possess by Thy Lordship, enjoy in Thy Good-
pleasure. Yea, even while swaddled as babes in
fleshly bands, Thy faithful servants being already
joined to Thee, do already latently and potentially
behold, know, choose, inherit, keep festival. The
vigil of Thy Feast excels the high days of time; the
threshold of Thy House, the presence-chamber of

earth's palaces: "I had rather be a doorkeeper in the house of my God, than to dwell in the tents of ungodliness". Or if as yet it be not thus with any, with me, Lord, make it thus to be with us all before we go hence and be no more seen. Amen.'

This commentary abounds in such fine prayers and in litanies, some much longer than the following characteristic short one:

From any sword that would devour for ever,
                    Lord, guard us.
From any hunger which Thou wilt not fill with good
    things,
                    Lord, guard us.
From any sickness unto death and not for Thy glory,
                    Lord, guard us.
From evil beasts,
                    Lord, guard us.
From the venomous crooked serpent, from the roaring lion, from the dragon and his angels,
                    Lord, guard us.

Here we must remember that Christina Rossetti means by 'evil beasts' the evil, sinful passions and the instruments of cruelty and lust who minister to Satan. Besides the prayers and litanies which make a chain of 'linked sweetness' all through *The Face of the Deep* there are also, as I have said before, some fine lyrics (now included in the *Poetical Works*).

In *Time Flies* and *Called to be Saints* we have examples of quite a different kind of writing, one that in minute observation and picturesque vision does bear a certain resemblance to Dorothy Wordsworth's descriptive passages and to the authoress' own poetry; take, for instance, this lovely musical description of the harebell in *Called to be Saints*:

The Bluebell or Harebell is a lovely small summer flower, mounted on a slim stalk and often hanging poised as if ready to tinkle. So slender is its growth, that one might fancy "harebell" no more than "hair-bell" misspelt. A clapperless bell it is, of a fine heavenly azure, trembling in each breeze which overtakes it on down, or heath, or hedgebank.

Or again:

So sweet are Violets, that truly Violet is but a second name for sweetness. On mossy banks, under hedgerows, overtopped by a fern or even by a blade of grass, curtained also among its own heart-shaped leaves, springs the Violet; which, not sufficed by a lowly stature, crooks downwards also the neck of its slender flower-stalk. Shades of blue-purple darker or lighter and passing into whiteness make its blossom comely, whereof a speck of gold lights up the centre....

...The petals having dropped away, the seed-vessel matures, and exhibits the figure of a somewhat irregularly-modelled globe; this, surrounded by the fingers of a five-pointed calyx, seems a miniature world held in the hollow of a hand.

And so on—writing that shows the minute care for the scientific detail of the botanist as well as the artist's sympathy for beauty of tint or shape. This minute care for detail in the delicate moulding of flowers, their shading and harmonies is matched by an attention no less meticulously fine for the beauties of precious stones. Jewels and flowers certainly played important parts in Christina Rossetti's underlying world of consciousness and were to her significant in the somewhat mystical sense that water was. Her choice of precious stones together with plants or creatures as the emblems of her saints shows, indeed, that she possessed in a high degree the sacramental instinct, the sense of all things material signifying something spiritual; of the senses as being merely channels through which are conveyed to the soul spiritual and intellectual lights. Of the emerald she says:

It seems no wonder that to the Emerald's alleged visual influence has been added a fancied power of conferring foreknowledge; besides which, eloquence and wealth have been supposed within the gift of this gem. And what saith our Blessed Lord to us? 'Behold, I have foretold you all things.'—*St Mark* xiii. 23.

Again, in *Seek and Find* she speaks thus of the wind:

What God brings out of His treasury cannot but be a treasure: our treasure if He blesses it to us. Amen.

Precious and beneficent is wind in the material world. It stirs up, purifies, winnows, casts aside: it is antagonistic to stagnation, to corruption: it brings heat, and likewise cold; it carries clouds, and dries up humidity. Invisible, intangible, audible, sensible, it has a breath so gentle as scarcely to bend a flower, and a blast stronger than the strength of the sea, stronger than the strength of the solid earth.

Turning to *Time Flies* we come to a homelier, a very human and domestic side of Christina Rossetti. There is humour with not a little dryness in it and much good common sense. On 21st February, for instance, we come to this remark

'A square man in a round hole',—we behold him incompatible, irreconcilable, a standing incongruity.

This world is full of square men in round holes; of persons unsuited to their post, calling, circumstances.

What is our square man to do? Clearly one of two things: he must either get out of his round hole, or else he must stay in it.

If he can get out by any lawful exit, let him up and begone, and betake himself to a square habitat.

But for one cubic man who can shift quarters, there may be a million who cannot....

Our permanent square tenant, then: what shall he do to mitigate the misfit which cannot be rectified?...

For 26th August the entry begins:

A nest implies, suggests, so much.

A circumference in comfortable proportion to its inhabitants' size.

Warmth and softness: 'For so He giveth His beloved sleep'.

Pure air, bright sunshine; leafy shade sufficient to satisfy a very Jonah.

A windy branch whereon to rock safely. Wind and rain heard yet little felt. A storm, indeed, sometimes, but as the exception not as the rule.

Most of all by way of comfort a nest suggests an overhanging presence of love. A brooding breast sheltering its cherished nestlings. A love ready to confront death in their defence.

'While we were yet sinners, Christ died for us.'

When 'room' and way are too great for us, let us think of Him Who prepared our present 'nest' and carries His little ones, and Who desires to see in each of us of the travail of His Soul and to be satisfied....

This is one of the best examples I can find of the homely-poetic, symbolic, yet practical nature of Christina Rossetti's devotional writing. Too often one feels that her awe at the majesty of the divine themes which she is contemplating constrains her to write with a certain stiffness.

For those days on which no saint's life is recorded she had to think of some little incident or anecdote prompted by the free working of her memory; many of these are very graceful indeed, besides throwing sidelights of much interest to her admirers. An entry for 16th September runs as follows:

Once as we descended a mountain side by side with the mountain torrent, my companion saw, while I missed seeing, a foambow.

In all my life I do not recollect to have seen one, except perhaps in artificial fountains; but such general omission seems a matter of course, and therefore simply a matter of indifference. That single natural foambow which I might have beheld and espied not, is the one to which may attach a tinge of regret; because, in a certain sense, it depended upon myself to look at it, yet I did not look.

I might have done so, and I did not: such is the sting to-day in petty matters.

And what else will be the sting in matters all important at the last day?

On 28th April she tells of a friend's painstaking observation of the work of spiders, and remarks:

I walked a little about the same country, and failed to observe the spider. Fortunately for me I was not a fly.

On 29th April she is dwelling in breathless delight upon the marvel of the cobweb:

It exhibits beauty, ingenuity, intricacy. Imagine it in the early morning jewelled with dewdrops, and each of these at sunny moments a spark of light or a section of rainbow. Woven, too, as no man could weave it, fine and flexible, frail and tenacious.

The *Letters* are best read together with the Biography by Mr Mackenzie Bell and *Time Flies*, the most personal and anecdotal of her prose works. They are not, as I have already said, very expansive, not even, considering by whom they were written, interesting letters (except to those who desire to collect any and every impression of Christina Rossetti). They are a little prim; a little reserved, and there are in them only small touches of imagination, though the humour is pretty frequently in play, while a delightful reality and an unaffected affection are their invariable accompaniments. Those written to Dante Gabriel and William Rossetti are the most revealing of her true nature. On 11th August, 1883, she wrote to her brother William from Birchington-on-Sea:

My dear William,

Thank you affectionately for the dear... letter of this morning. As yours was virtually and primarily to our Mother, so this is to all intents and purposes from her.

There is one superb virtue in which you and she alike shine and in which—at least by comparison—I fear I only glimmer,—justice. She, with unvarying love to you, will not hear of any arrangement which either in fact or appearance displaces you from your proper and dominant position as controller of the monument. She therefore absolutely withdraws her late suggestion; and, enshrining her own pious hope in her own window, awaits the monument under such an aspect as you assign to it. *Therefore* do not ask either of us to write to F. M. B., for direct from you and from you only will he receive instructions.... She wrote to you yesterday, and doubtless you already have her letter. And I add, as knowing it positively, that her secession from the monument-question is according to her own absolute and deliberate wish, and creates neither sore nor chill in that glowing maternal heart....

This extract from a characteristic letter shows that
Christina Rossetti had a somewhat conventional
form of address. Polite, reserved even, with those to
whom she was most deeply attached, and meticulously, scrupulously just. The monument alluded to
is the memorial to Dante Gabriel Rossetti at Birchington-on-Sea—an Irish cross designed by Ford
Madox Brown. A letter which shows her lighter vein
is her comment on the drawing by Dante Gabriel to
which I have already referred (p. 25). In his intro-
ductory note William Rossetti explains that it 'is
headed by a primitive portrayal of two hands raised
in astonishment and a note of admiration', and that
'the Henrietta here mentioned was Henrietta Poly-
dore, daughter of our uncle; she was at this time
aged 16 or thereabouts'.

81 High Street, Hastings,
(December 1864).

My dear Gabriel,

Such is my attitude vis-à-vis of the historic
record of my finished work. The stolid equanimity
of the elephant under the loss of his trunk is perhaps
my favourite point: though Henrietta justly directed
my admiration to the rueful eye which the chip
directs to the old block (head).

A Miss Smith has asked and obtained Mac's leave
to melodise one of my things, I know not which.
The other day a Rev. Mr Baines wrote begging my
permission for him to reprint *House to Home*, in a

collection he is preparing to promote a charitable object: after consulting Mac I consented. Jean Ingelow is in his list of contributors; and Dean Alford, not that I rate him very high poetically.

Uncle Henry and Henrietta join in love.

Lastly we come to a couple of short novels (chronologically these take early rank among her works) and a handful of stories which were either written for church magazines, etc., or for children.

Maude, the first novel, has a certain wistful power. It portrays a delicate young girl, a poetess of some promise, who dies young. *Commonplace* is more elaborate and a little more advanced in technique, and the study of the home life of the three sisters depicted in it reveals possibilities of a dramatic power to come. Not here, however, was she to find herself, not in these dim chequered drawing-rooms, these veiled, platitudinous societies; she was not to become a feminine Trollope, even a Mrs Oliphant— nor could she aspire to be a Mrs Gaskell.

Of the short stories, those written for children and concerning animals have most vivacity and charm about them. The descriptions of Maggie's awful dreams are vivid: one could not easily forget 'a glutinous-looking girl in pink cotton velvet'. *Hero* is a kind of fairy story in which there are touches of magic and colour faintly suggestive of the author's poetic capabilities. But on the whole Christina Rossetti's attempts at story writing are the least interesting things she did.

Indeed, in spite of her faculty for prose, of which Professor Saintsbury calls her 'an exquisite mistress', none of her work in this medium can ever be set beside the glory of her poems. Such things as 'Birds of Paradise', 'Songs in a Cornfield', 'Sleep at Sea' and 'Twice' (beginning 'I took my heart in my hand') came easily and were easily of the best in their kind. *Seek and Find, The Face of the Deep* and the other fine prose books live mainly on account of the wonderful uprushing of lyrical poetry that is in them. They are like marsh beds silently filled with waters—the waters spring up here and there with a welcome bubbling of music and gladden both the ear and the eye by their glittering joyful beauty and their godly rhythm. A poet she was first and last, and one is grateful for the knowledge that as such she discerned herself, and as such she was recognised during her lifetime.

Chapter Four

CHRISTINA ROSSETTI IN THE PATTERN OF HER TIME

> By the waters of Babylon
>   We thirst for Jordan yet,
> We pine for Jerusalem
>   Whereon our hearts are set.
> > (*From 'By the Waters of Babylon'*)

The age of Queen Victoria was one of energy, quick action, the bursting forth of pent-up powers, vivacious enterprise, glorious as the age of Queen Elizabeth in dreams, splendid with courage, noble with humanitarian, religious, scientific, moral, artistic and poetic zeal. To know only a little of the principal literature of this reign is to know things astonishingly various, contradictory in outlook but alike in one amazing sense—their common quality of courage.

Courage rings in the 'Last Word' of Matthew Arnold.

> They out-talk'd thee, hiss'd thee, tore thee,
> Better men fared thus before thee;
> Fired their ringing shot and pass'd,
> Hotly charged—and broke at last.

> Charge once more, then, and be dumb!
> Let the victors, when they come,
> When the forts of folly fall,
> Find thy body by the wall.

Courage is the very colour of Browning's rich and royal mind; 'I was ever a fighter' would have been a fitting line to put upon his tombstone. Courage nerved the fragile Mrs Browning to cut the cords— cruel, unjust cords—that bound her to invalidism and a home without happiness, to throw out sympathy with oppressed and suffering peoples everywhere, and to live singing and celebrating the joy she found in a noble and human sense through her perfect marriage, her motherhood, her art. Courage embued Ruskin, William Morris, Newman, Darwin, Swinburne and Matthew Arnold; to take only a handful of the great names which are among the chief glories of this remarkable renaissance. It is true that Newman and Darwin, William Morris and Matthew Arnold differed in their aims, and that their philosophies might not harmonise; it is true that they were workers in varied fields, but they had courage in common, they were at once venturers and men of strong social consciousness, seeking the good of the future, concerned for truth and for goodness. To William Morris, in the heyday of his life, when his Oxford dreams of founding a monastery had faded into broad daylight, goodness could not be imagined without social and practical effort. 'If a chap can't write poetry whilst he is weaving tapestry, he had better shut up' he once said. *The*

Earthly Paradise was no faint mirage with him, and his 'Psyche in robe of mystic blue' might have been the vision he had of the new soul which was to arise from the old sheath when the looms of England should be heard humming again and her casks be swollen with home-brewed cider. That England of his was to be what Blake foretold and dreamed of, 'The New Jerusalem'. William Morris in *A Dream of John Ball* set his lesser but still noble imagination to contrive the actual story of an Utopia; but Blake had been the prophet whose voice's echo was still heard passionately denouncing cruelty and praying that health and holiness might take their root and be enthroned 'in England's green and pleasant land'.

To the Oxford reformers the dream of bringing about the regeneration, the encrownment of their beloved country, took another shape. To them it seemed that it was the angel of faith alone who, by blowing his golden trumpet across the yellow corn-fields and the silver pastures, and by restoring the thought of sacramental worship in the little half-deserted country churches, could bring about the reconciliation between Man and 'God, our Father dear' whose 'Child and care' Man is. To them it would be the mystic presence of our Lord and Saviour, Jesus Christ, upon the altar of each little

grey and greenly secluded church in every hamlet
or in every town or village, that must touch the
springs of love and pity, whereby the world which
was growing out into so many impulsive directions,
elaborating so many mechanical devices, spreading
the black and blood-red arms of its industrial enterprise with such ruthless force and determination,
could be chastened, comforted, uplifted.

To some of these men, including Newman their
leader, the thought came that such a rounding up
at the call of the angel-clarion of faith could not
logically be made unless historically false foundations
be renounced, a certain submission and a turning
back to retrace steps accomplished, and a certain
join cemented: only thus could any efforts to restore
true religious sentiments in this country bear fruit.
Be this how it may, numbers of quite disinterested
and just-minded high churchmen looked differently
at the question; and Keble, one of the poets whose
work should be studied close to Miss Rossetti's,
Isaac Williams too, with the devout Dr Pusey—and
numerous others—remained in the Church of England, but did much to requicken the lamps of personal devotion and the somewhat shy spirituality
that had marvellously survived a long period of
decay in national Church life.

This strong though slender tributary to the spirit

of the later part of Queen Victoria's reign is not at all really a contradictory one. It made many converts both to the Catholic movement within the Church of England and to the older Church herself. Among such converts and devotees we look for and find the names of several poets. Christina Rossetti was one of those who believed in the Puseyite Movement, and if we wish entirely to understand her mind and her relation to other writers of her day we ought to take full account of this. She was thus in the strictest sense not without modern sympathies. Although she was not of a scientific turn, her interest in the sea shore, the hedgerow, or the night sky, led her into reading about nature and studying her with minute and reverent care.

In temperament she was sensitively and deeply moral—hardly so much ethical as moral—in which differentiation we see her divided from Mrs Browning, from George Eliot and from Ruskin. She shrank from active participation in the 'Woman's Movement' rather as she shrank from the thought of scientific experiments that might lead to cruelty or agnosticism (her horror at vivisection was profound and abiding). Without the smallest ostentation she was a devoted friend of poor people; all that was hurt, obscure, weak and humble *claimed* her heart. (It is said of her that she preferred ungainly or awkward animals to those dowered with much beauty and grace.) In all this she was a true daughter of the age of pity, the age that sought to build the 'New Jerusalem' and to seek the face of 'God our Father dear'. She would have nothing to do with commercialism, but she was alive to the sufferings of all those caught in its toils.

And then we must not forget that this shy and retiring woman was in close touch with many of the best artists and thinkers of her day, and that she shared the glory of poetry with Swinburne, who seems always to have reverenced her utterly and of whom she wrote with frank, sympathetic admiration.[1] Her literary as well as her human relation to her brother, Gabriel Rossetti, was one of final satisfaction to both. In both there was a spirituality that, like Blake's, loved mercy and generosity and knew where to look for these things. Both had the vision which transcends materialism, in that it gives to every substance its true spiritual value and sees, as Francis Thompson saw, mystically—in and through the light of the eyes—not intellectually, and that looks beyond the form and substance of things; 'Turn but a stone and start a wing'. To Christina

---

[1] It will, of course, be remembered that W. M. Rossetti dedicated the volume of Christina's poems called *New Poems* to Swinburne, whom he calls a 'generous eulogist'.

Rossetti it was natural to write of angels, of robins too, or of dormice and sea anemones. No one of these beings could leap out of its natural sphere and become something else; each had its right place in the mystical circles and was thus seen to bear a spiritual importance the greater for its clearly defined position in the eternal harmony. She kept things in their right niches, and she handled each and all with the sure touch which belongs to a poet of this kind, who will never be incoherent or muddled.

It is this clearness of vision which is so inimitable both in her work and that of her brother. Their own particular gifts had surety in common, a distinct directness and a power of going straight wherever they meant to; whether they soared up into Paradise or dived beneath the sea. From 'The Blessed Damozel' I quote an instance of this ease:

> From the fixed place of Heaven she saw
> > Time like a pulse shake fierce
> Through all the worlds. Her gaze still strove
> > Within the gulf to pierce
> Its path; and now she spoke as when
> > The stars sang in their spheres.

Or again one may find the same at-homeness in the literal element of golden air and fire, where none can

breathe save poets of this soaring and ethereal order
in these lines from the 'Last Confession':

> ...As if a window had been opened in heaven,
> For God to give His blessing from, before
> This world of ours should set; (for in my dream
> I thought our world was setting, and the sun
> Flared, a spent taper;) and beneath that gust
> The rings of light quivered like forest-leaves.

'Our world was setting':—it is a remarkable figure:
awful and compressed, suggesting rather than out-
lining a most majestic and terrible spectacle. It
shows the mould of the poet's mind to have been
like that of his sister's—very literal, and yet grandly
other-worldly in that special sense in which only the
mind of an at-once visual and visionary artist can be.

In this they were in contrast to many of their
contemporaries: they had so rich an inheritance of
Catholic (implied) philosophy; they had the Latin
incisiveness and clear-cut picturesque sense of
concrete images, and they were again individual and
lonely in a day of large movements and sweeping
democratic gesture. For both the Rossettis colour
and music and spirit and sense must not merely meet
or even mingle, they must be united in poetry:

> She had cast away her jewels
>   And her rich attire,
> And her breast was filled with a holy shame.
>   And her heart with a holy fire.

So writes Christina of St Mary Magdalene. Again she says of 'the dead bride':

> There she lay so still and pale,
>   With her bridal robes around her:
> Joy is fleeting, life is frail,
>   Death had found her.

Another bond that bound these two poets was a leaning they held in common towards mystery, towards the grave, to ghostly visions, and the haunting of springs and woods:

> There are sleeping dreams and waking dreams;
> What seems is not always as it seems.

These opening lines from the strange vision of three symbolical ships called 'A Ballad of Boding' have almost the ring of Gabriel Rossetti's own verse; whilst these closing lines of a beautiful sonnet by her brother, called 'The Church Porch':

> Silence, and sudden dimness, and deep prayer,
>   And faces of crowned angels all about

have much of Christina's saintly and mystic light about them, bringing holy faces and wings at a touch within the compass of a rural and saddened setting.

> I have a friend in ghostland—
> Early found, ah me how early lost!—
> Blood-red seaweeds drip along that coastland
>   By the strong sea wrenched and tost.

> If I wake he hunts me like a nightmare:
>   I feel my hair stand up, my body creep:
> Without light I see a blasting sight there,
>   See a secret I must keep.[1]

To such moods of reflected dreamlight and occasionally eerie vision Christina strongly inclined. Religion being, however, her paramount care, selected duty and chosen path, she was careful to guard with jealous zeal against any of her lesser and purely fantastic inclinations to stray too far along these flowery dream-haunted walks, or to wander too deeply amidst the murmurous blossoming glades, whose fruit is like that of the Goblins—perilously sweet.

She had not, as had Mrs Browning, any inclination towards psychical investigation; indeed, she took the view always voiced by orthodox religion in strongly condemning any such tampering with the unseen—any such trafficking with things that may at least prove unwholesome and are more than likely to prove unholy would have seemed to her to be a grave sin in a Christian.

> Oh my soul, she beats her wings
>   And pants to fly away
> Up to immortal things
>   In the heavenly day

[1] *A Nightmare*, a fragment by Christina Rossetti.

are the lines which best sum up her aspirations. However prone she was to follow a certain delicate waywardness of fancy—her soul, her heart and her mind were anchored firmly, her sails were blown by no chance wind.

With a difference, this is of course essentially true of Dante Gabriel Rossetti. All his noblest poetry escapes the danger of being merely ornamental, macabre, or sensuous; the best of it has that heavenly flame-like quality of 'The Blessed Damozel' or that piercing pity for innocence betrayed which is shed around the youthful 'Jenny' before her tragedy, who used to

> ...lie in fields and look
> Along the ground through the blown grass,
> And wonder where the city was.

In this essential right-mindedness which in spite of the aberrations of his sick body always remained with Rossetti the poet-painter, he was as much a son of the age which sought to redress wrongs and bring beauty to the doorsteps of the poor, as any of the more conscious exponents of social reform.

No one had a more passionate sense of the responsibility of life than had this pair of poets, a brother and a sister, so widely separated by temperament and habit, but yet so deeply alike in pure intention and first-born reaction to things of beauty and of moral value. And it is good to think that where in life the links that bound them together were of necessity strained by the usage of much misery, in the artistic reputation and in the immortality which they shared these links never can be broken. Just as in the work of the Brownings we have the poetry of a husband and wife flowing and interflowing until their very unlikeness becomes merged in a sort of strange unity and sweet accord of common assent; so with the two Rossettis, a brother and a sister, we have an accord, a harmony which flows from the same fount outward into different but never into alien channels.

It will be seen from the foregoing description of Christina Rossetti's poetry, and also of her life, that I have laid stress upon her unique powers and those of her brother; nevertheless it cannot be said too strongly that the age in which they worked, although varied and bristling with individualities of all kinds, had amongst others one great common faculty, namely, the love of sensuous beauty. If we open Christina Rossetti's poetry or Dante Gabriel's anywhere—if we open by chance our Browning, our William Morris, what shall we find? We shall as likely as not find some exquisite descriptive passage which has melody as well as colour and is satisfying